Slippery, Slimy

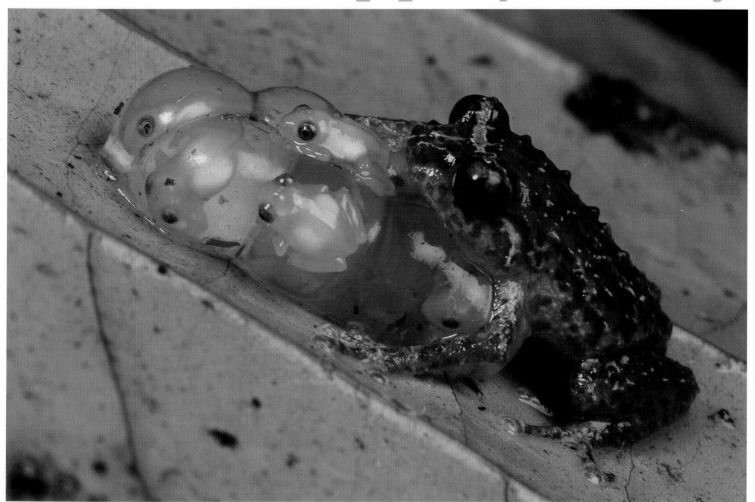

BABY FROGS

Sandra Markle

Walker & Company ✸ New York

You may not have seen a baby frog like this Monkey Tree Frog baby from Peru. But frogs live in all parts of the world except Antarctica. So nearly everywhere, baby frogs of one kind or another can be spotted in streams, in ponds, in puddles—even in tiny pools of water trapped in a plant's leaves. They can also be found in a foam nest in a tree, in a pouch on their mother's back, or inside their father's mouth. So how does a baby frog live? How does it stay safe? And what kinds of changes happen as it grows up? This book gives you a close look at baby frogs—also known as "tadpoles."

rogs belong to a group of animals called *amphibians* (am-FIB-ee-anz). The name means "leading two lives." They're called that because adult frogs and baby frogs look and behave very differently. Adults, like this Gray Tree Frog, can stay out of water at least part of the time. That's why adult frogs are built to jump as well as swim. And adults have *lungs* to extract *oxygen,* the gas they need to live, from the air.

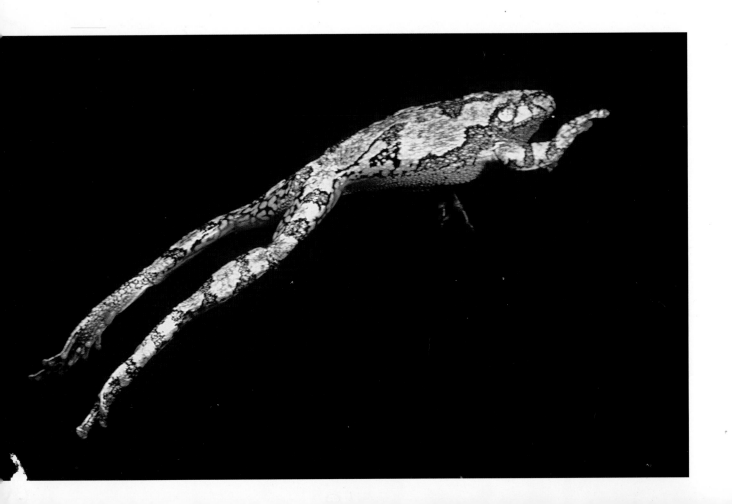

Baby frogs, like this Red-eyed Tree Frog tadpole, can live only in water. That's why tadpoles are fish-shaped—to be good swimmers. Like fish, baby frogs also have *gills* to extract the oxygen they need from the water.

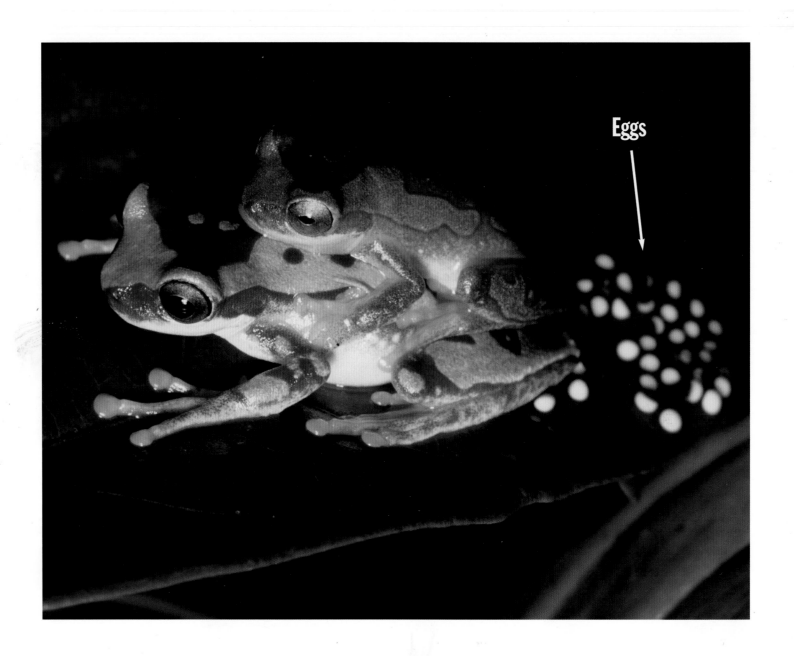

Eggs

STARTING LIFE IN AN EGG

These Hourglass Tree Frogs are mating. To produce babies, a female frog lays *eggs*. Then the male covers the eggs with a liquid containing special cells, called *sperm*. When a sperm merges with an egg, a baby frog starts to develop.

Each newly laid frog egg is inside a jellylike blob. The outer surface of this jelly forms a rubbery shell. But water is able to pass through this shell. When the jelly gets wet, it quickly swells to nearly twice its size. This thick layer of jelly becomes a protective covering for the egg. It keeps the egg from being bumped and from getting too hot or too cold. As long as the jelly stays wet, it also lets oxygen pass through to the developing baby frog. Even inside the egg, the baby frog needs oxygen to live and grow. So frog parents make sure their eggs stay wet.

Many frogs, like Bullfrogs, keep their eggs wet simply by laying them in water. Other frogs, like these Foam Nest Frogs, produce a special coating to keep their eggs from drying out. Foam Nest Frogs mate in a group up in a tree. During mating, the females give off a thick, sticky liquid and whip it with their hind legs until it's like stiff egg whites. The females deposit their eggs inside the group's foam nest. Soon the surface of the foam hardens into a protective case. This keeps the eggs inside moist and soft. Because the foam bubbles contain trapped air, there is a supply of oxygen for the developing babies.

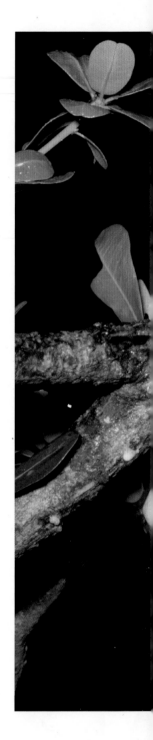

Some frogs, like this *Phrynopus* (fry-NOP-us) female, lay their eggs on the ground in a place that's nearly always damp, like under moss. She stays nearby, regularly peeing on the eggs to keep them wet while the babies develop.

Pygmy Marsupial (PIG-mee mar-SOOP-e-ul) Frogs have a special way to keep their eggs wet. The lumps on this female Pygmy Marsupial Frog's back are her eggs. When she mated, the male frog coated the eggs with sperm and pushed them into a pouch on her back. Now, while she goes about finding food and staying safe, the *mucus* produced by her *skin* keeps the eggs wet.

Many kinds of frogs don't stay with their eggs or guard them. So those frog parents usually produce lots of eggs. Bullfrogs, for example, produce as many as 12,000 eggs each time they mate. That way, if a hunter eats some of the eggs, there are still likely to be some left.

This Cat-eyed Snake is dining on Red-eyed Tree Frog eggs. Tadpoles will soon develop inside any eggs the snake doesn't eat. When these baby frogs hatch, they'll drop into the stream below. Of course, there are hungry hunters in the water too. Fish, turtles, and water insects all eat baby frogs. So, once they hatch, baby frogs have to work at staying safe in order to grow up.

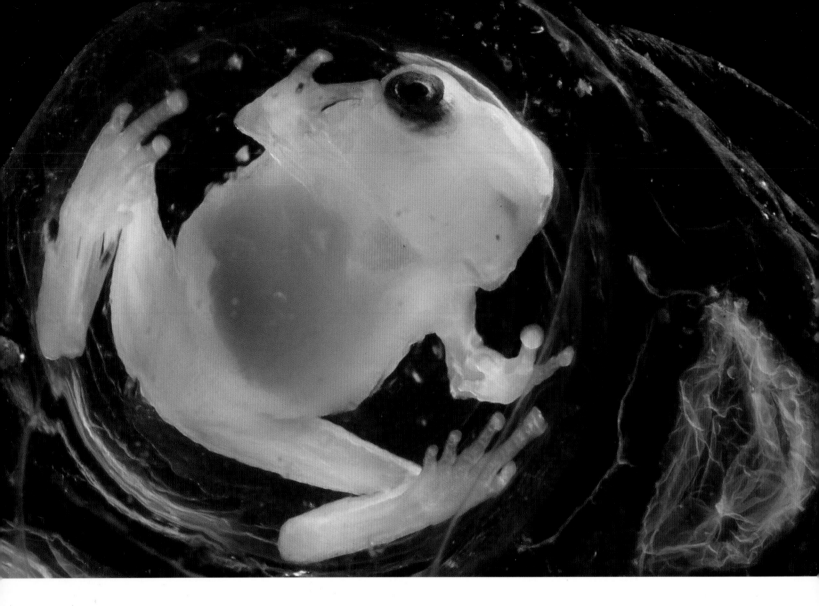

Two Ways to Grow Up

The bodies of all baby frogs change shape and function as they develop into adults. Some, like these Narrow-mouthed Frogs, change directly from a ball of cells into their adult form. Then the young adult frogs hatch.

Most, though, go through a tadpole stage. Take a close look at these Foam Nest Frog tadpoles. Each time a tadpole hatches, the liquid inside its egg spills into the foam nest. Because there are lots of eggs in a nest, hundreds of tadpoles hatch at the same time. So all the spilled liquid softens the dried foam. Drip! Drop! The softened bits of nest and the tadpoles start to drop out of the tree. That's why the frog parents stuck their nest to a branch just above the surface of a stream. The tadpoles land in the water. They'll finish growing up there.

On Their Own

Because most adult frogs leave their eggs once they are laid, most baby frogs grow up without parents. Some, like these Leaf Frog tadpoles, stay safe by remaining close to their brothers and sisters. Hunters are less likely to pick individuals out of a big group.

Some tadpoles have special features that help them stay safe. Torrent (TOR-ent) Frog tadpoles have really big lips. To stay alive, the tadpoles swim into the fastest-flowing part of the stream. Then they press their lips against rocks and use their mouths like suction cups to hold on. Carried along by the stream's rushing current, hungry fish zip past the tadpoles too fast to attack.

Baby Hourglass Tree Frogs appear to develop special body features only if they need them. So tadpoles living in ponds where there are few hungry hunters have skinny, see-through tails. But tadpoles living in ponds with lots of enemies look different. Those baby Hourglass Tree Frogs have thick, dark tails. Such a showy tail could distract an enemy. A baby frog could still grow up if all it lost were part of its tail. Losing its head would be another story.

TAKING CARE OF BABY

Some baby frogs do get special care from their parents while they're growing up. This Strawberry Poison Dart Frog mother is giving her tadpole a ride to a special nursery—a pool of rainwater trapped in a plant's leaves. The mucus on her skin helps the baby frog hold on. Then she'll carry her other tadpoles, one at a time, to different nurseries. And her care doesn't end there. Every few days, the mother frog visits each of her tadpoles. While there, she produces a few eggs to deposit in the tadpole's pool. These eggs provide the baby frog with the food it needs to grow and change into an adult.

These young Darwin's Frogs have just hopped out of their father's mouth! During mating, the female lays about fifteen large eggs on top of damp leaves on the forest floor. The male stays close by, peeing on them to keep them wet until they hatch. Then he scoops the tadpoles into his mouth, where they slip into his *vocal sac,* the stretchy pouch covering his throat. For about two months, Dad gets on with his life, catching bugs to eat, while the tadpoles grow bigger. The baby frogs live on the food energy in the egg yolk they absorbed before they hatched. He can't make a sound with the tadpoles in his vocal sac, so having his brood become adults and hop out really gives him something to croak about!

These Hip Pocket Frog tadpoles are climbing up their father's legs. After the parents mate, the female deposits her eggs on leaf litter and leaves. Dad stands guard for about ten days, until the tadpoles hatch. Then he sits down in the middle of his brood so the tadpoles can wiggle into one of the pouches on his big hind legs. Although the female lays about twenty eggs, there is room only for about six tadpoles in each pouch. So only the strongest and fastest survive. Inside the pouches, the tadpoles grow and develop for about two months, living on the energy left from their egg yolks. When they change into young adults, they pop out of the pouches and hop away.

A baby frog that goes through a tadpole stage must change its shape to become an adult. It must also change the way its body works. While those changes don't happen all at once, most tadpoles become young adults in just a few months. Tadpoles in puddles that are drying up or those with a limited food supply change faster. The Strawberry Poison Dart Frog tadpole, growing up in its tiny rainwater pool, changes into an adult in just three weeks. On the other hand, a Bullfrog tadpole living in a big pond with plenty of food takes as long as fourteen months to become an adult. Even water temperature can affect how long it takes for tadpoles to develop— the colder the water, the longer it will take.

Fast or slow, the process of change is the same. Look closely at how this Wood Frog tadpole changes into an adult. One of the earliest changes is that bumps form and become hind legs.

Next, the tadpole grows front legs. Inside, its body is changing too. For one thing, the baby frog develops lungs. When the lungs take over the job of supplying oxygen, the young frog pokes its head out of the water and takes its first breath.

Soon the tadpole's fishlike body changes into its adult shape. Once eyelids develop, the youngster can blink. And the fishlike lips and mouth change into an adult frog's wide mouth and long tongue. Now the youngster is able to catch and digest insects.

Changing from a tadpole to a young adult frog takes lots of energy. Besides getting energy from the food it eats, the developing youngster uses up the food energy stored in its tail, making the tail shrink. Even before it's completely gone, though, the baby frog is ready for its life as an adult.

Where in the World Are These Frogs?

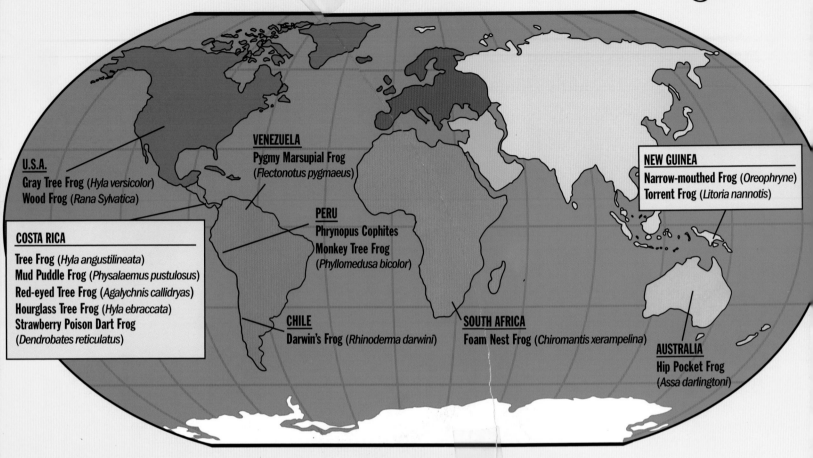

VENEZUELA
Pygmy Marsupial Frog
(*Flectonotus pygmaeus*)

NEW GUINEA
Narrow-mouthed Frog (*Oreophryne*)
Torrent Frog (*Litoria nannotis*)

U.S.A.
Gray Tree Frog (*Hyla versicolor*)
Wood Frog (*Rana Sylvatica*)

PERU
Phrynopus Cophites
Monkey Tree Frog
(*Phyllomedusa bicolor*)

COSTA RICA
Tree Frog (*Hyla angustilineata*)
Mud Puddle Frog (*Physalaemus pustulosus*)
Red-eyed Tree Frog (*Agalychnis callidryas*)
Hourglass Tree Frog (*Hyla ebraccata*)
Strawberry Poison Dart Frog
(*Dendrobates reticulatus*)

CHILE
Darwin's Frog (*Rhinoderma darwini*)

SOUTH AFRICA
Foam Nest Frog (*Chiromantis xerampelina*)

AUSTRALIA
Hip Pocket Frog
(*Assa darlingtoni*)

While the frogs you discovered in this book may also be found in other parts of the world, check the map to see where they were photographed.

In some parts of the world, frogs that were once common are now becoming rare. Researchers aren't sure why this is happening. Some suggest it's due to climate changes and diseases. Others think the cause is chemicals getting into the water, or wetlands being drained. More than likely, frog populations are being hurt by all of these things. Find out what kinds of frogs live in your area. Are any in trouble? If so, learn what is being done to protect them, and how your family can help. Then go to work to help save the frogs.

Raise Your Own Baby Frogs

Do frogs live in ponds or streams near you? If so, take some eggs home to watch them hatch and see the tadpoles change into frogs. Just follow these steps to care for the growing tadpoles. Then return the young frogs to the same place you collected the eggs. (Note: If frog populations in your area are shrinking, leave the eggs where you find them. Then visit every few days to look for tadpoles and see young adults emerge.)

1. Collect the eggs in a clean plastic container with a snap-on lid. Scoop up some water too so they don't dry out on the way home.

2. Put the eggs in a clean plastic or glass container with a wide opening. A fish bowl is perfect.

3. Fill the container with bottled water to be sure there are no chemicals, like chlorine and ammonia, which are bad for the baby frogs.

4. Add aquatic plants (available at stores that sell aquarium supplies). This will feed the tadpoles.

5. Lower the water level as soon as the tadpoles start to sprout legs. Also add rocks rinsed in bottled water so the young adults can climb. The frogs now need to breathe air.

6. Return the young frogs to their home as soon as their tails disappear.

GLOSSARY/INDEX

AMPHIBIAN [am-FIB-ee-an] A group of animals with gilled young that live in water and air-breathing adults that live at least part of the time on land. **4**

EGG [eg] The name given to the female reproductive cell. It is also the name given to the fertilized egg that will produce a baby frog. **7, 8, 10, 11, 13, 15, 16, 21, 22, 24**

GILL [gil] The body part in which oxygen is extracted from the water. **5**

LUNG [lung] The body part in which oxygen is extracted from the air. **4, 28**

MUCUS [MEW-kus] A thick, slippery fluid produced to moisten and protect the body part, such as the frog's skin, that produces it. **11, 21**

OXYGEN [AHK-sih-jen] A gas in the air and water that passes into the tadpole's blood through the gills and into the adult's body through the lungs. The blood then carries it around the body, where it is combined with food to release energy. **4, 5, 7, 8, 28**

SKIN [skin] The outer protective covering of a frog's body. **11**

SPERM [spurm] The male reproductive cell. When the sperm joins with the female's egg, a baby frog develops. **7, 11**

VOCAL SAC [VOH-kul sak] A pouchlike part in some kinds of male frogs. It swells up when the frog forces air from its lungs through it to produce sounds. **22**

With love for Emily Sims McGrinder and her daughters: Kelly, Katie, Maura, Meghan, Molly, and Colleen

My favorite part of creating *Slippery, Slimy Baby Frogs* was finding the photos. Tracking down and contacting frog experts around the world was a detective job. I talked to one expert, through a satellite link, while he was deep in a Peruvian rain forest. After producing more than sixty photo-essays, I've made friends with many gifted wildlife photographers who spend their lives traveling to remote places and enduring difficult conditions to capture fantastic, once-in-a-lifetime shots. I'm delighted to share the images they work so hard to capture on film. Take another look at the photos in *Slippery, Slimy Baby Frogs* and you'll see a unique peek at young frogs taken by people who have made great efforts to study and photograph them.

First published in the United States of America in 2006 by Walker Publishing Company, Inc.
Distributed to the trade by Holtzbrinck Publishers

For information about permission to reproduce selections from this book, write to Permissions, Walker & Company, 104 Fifth Avenue, New York, New York 10011

Library of Congress Cataloging-in-Publication Data

Markle, Sandra.
Slippery, slimy baby frogs / Sandra Markle.
   p. cm.
ISBN-10: 0-8027-8062-8 (hardcover)
ISBN-13: 978-0-8027-8062-1 (hardcover)
ISBN-10: 0-8027-8063-6 (reinforced)
ISBN-13: 978-0-8027-8063-8 (reinforced)
   1. Frogs—Infancy—Juvenile literature. I. Title.

QL668.E2M297 2006   597.8'9139—dc22
2005027542

Book design by Nicole Gastonguay

Visit Walker & Company's Web site at www.walkeryoungreaders.com

Printed in China

10 9 8 7 6 5 4 3 2 1

Acknowledgment:
I would especially like to thank the following people for sharing their expertise and enthusiasm: Dr. Klaus Busse, Zoologisches Forschungsinstitut and Museum; Alexander Koenig, Bonn, Germany; Dr. Alessandro Catenazzi, Department of Biological Sciences, Florida International University; and Dr. Heike Proehl, Assistant Professor at the Institute of Zoology, Veterinary School of Hanover, Germany, specializing in the behavioral ecology of frogs. A special thank you to my husband, Skip Jeffery, for his help and support through the creative process.

Photo Credits:
Alessandro Catenazzi 10
Michael and Patricia Fogden cover, 6, 11, 12, 15, 16, 19, 20, 23
George Grall 1, 3, 5, 14, 17
Skip Jeffery 30
Dwight Kuhn 4, 26, 28, 29
Michael Mahony 25

Exploring Music

Eunice Boardman   Beth Landis   Barbara Andress

illustrated by Kenneth Longtemps

Consultants

Milton Babbitt   Dorothy K. Gillett   Virginia Stroh Red
Keith E. Baird   Alan Lomax   Fela Sowande
Louis W. Ballard   Kurt Miller   Kurt Stone
Chou Wen-chung   Elena Paz   Nelmatilda Woodard

HOLT, RINEHART AND WINSTON, INC.
New York, Toronto, London, Sydney

Acknowledgments

Grateful acknowledgment is given to the following authors and publishers:

American Book Company for "Boom Dali Da" from *Expressing Music* by Choate, *et. al.*; for the words to "The Cowboy" from *The American Singer*, Second Edition, Book 2, by Beattie, Wolverton, Wilson and Hinga. Used by permission.

The Bodley Head for "Dog Jumps Through the Window" from *The Children's Song Book* by Elizabeth Poston. Used by permission.

Cooperative Recreation Service, Inc. for "Kokoleoko" and "Ingonyama" from *African Songs;* "Dipidu" from *Sing a Tune;* "Rique Ran" from *Songs and Games of South American Children;* "Hoot Owl Song" from *Homeland Songs;* "The Frogs" from *Rounds;* "Hold On" from *Look Away;* and "The Lotus" ("Hiraita") from *Japanese Songs.* Used by permission.

Crown Publishers, Inc. for "Little Car," taken from *A Book of Nonsense Songs*, edited by Norman Cazden. Copyright © 1961 by Norman Cazden. Melody and lyrics Copyright © 1961 by Melody Trails, Inc., New York, N.Y. Used by permission.

E. P. Dutton & Co., Inc. for "See Saw" by Evelyn Beyer and two verses of "Little Black Bug" by Margaret Wise Brown from the book *Another Here and Now Story Book* by Lucy Sprague Mitchell. Copyright 1937 by E. P. Dutton & Co., Inc. Renewal © 1965 by Lucy Sprague Mitchell. Used by permission.

General Music Publishing Company, Inc., for "I'll Sing You a Song" from *A Cat Came Fiddling.* Copyright by General Music Publishing Company, Inc. Used by permission.

Gulf Music Company for the music to "The Flag Goes By" by William S. Haynie. Copyright © 1966 by Gulf Music Company. Used by permission.

Harvard University Press for "All the Pretty Little Horses" from *On the Trail of Negro Folksongs* by Dorothy Scarborough. Copyright 1925 by Harvard University Press and 1953 by Mary McDaniel Parker. Used by permission.

Irving Lowens for the music to "Rain Song." Copyright by Irving Lowens. Used by permission.

David McKay Company, Inc. for "Sing, Sing, Sing." Copyright © 1961, 1969 by Beatrice Landeck. From *Echoes of Africa.* Used by permission.

G. Schirmer, Inc. for "The Angel Band" from *36 South Carolina Spirituals* by Carl Diton. Copyright 1930, © 1957 by G. Schirmer, Inc. For "Posheen, Posheen, Posho" by John Jacob Niles. Copyright 1953 by G. Schirmer, Inc. Used by permission.

Schmitt, Hall & McCreary Company for "The Cuckoo" from *Songs Children Sing.* Used by permission.

Schroder Music Co. for "Place to Be." Words and music by Malvina Reynolds. Copyright © 1961 by Schroder Music Co. (ASCAP). Used by permission.

Systems for Education, Inc. for "Rainy Day" by Virginia Stroh Red. Copyright © 1966 by Systems for Education, Inc. Used by permission.

The Viking Press, Inc. for the words to "Firefly" from *Under the Tree* by Elizabeth Madox Roberts. Copyright 1922 by B. W. Huebsch, Inc. Renewed 1950 by Ivor S. Roberts. Used by permission.

Walton Music Corporation for "Donkey Small," words by Marilyn Keith and Alan Bergman, and music by Norman Luboff. Copyright © 1957 by Walton Music Corporation, 1841 Broadway, New York, N.Y. Used by permission.

Additional copyright acknowledgments and photo credits appear with the materials used.

Music autography by Maxwell Weaner
Cover art by Norman Laliberté

Contents

Let's Explore Music

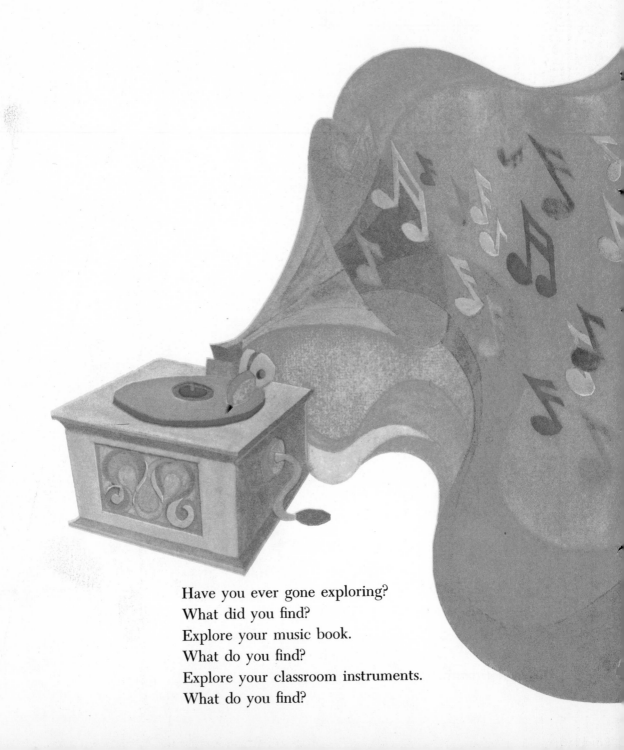

Have you ever gone exploring?
What did you find?
Explore your music book.
What do you find?
Explore your classroom instruments.
What do you find?

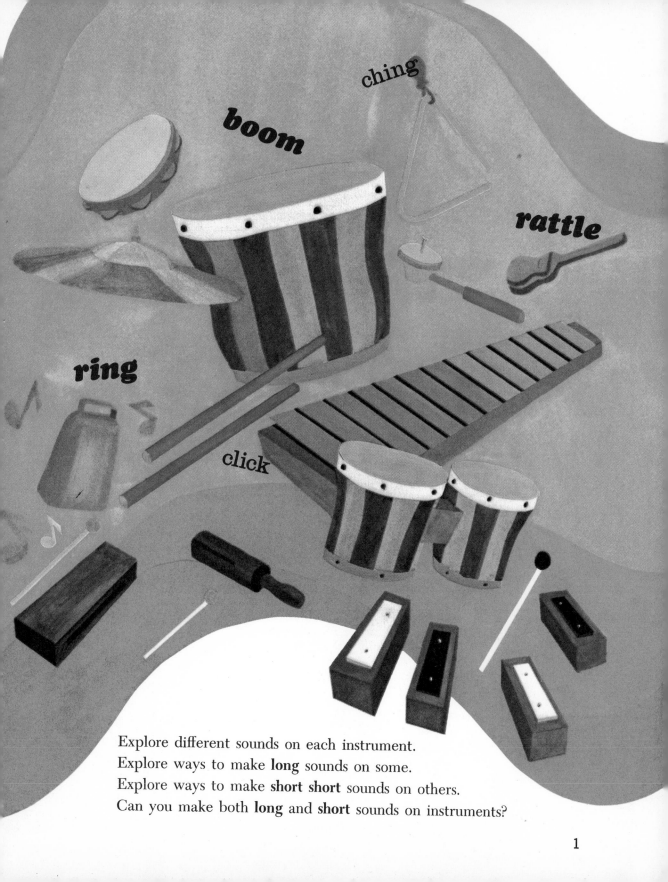

ching

boom

rattle

ring

click

Explore different sounds on each instrument.
Explore ways to make **long** sounds on some.
Explore ways to make **short short** sounds on others.
Can you make both **long** and **short** sounds on instruments?

1

Mister Monday

Words and Music by B.A.

Sing about each day of the week.
Play these bells over and over again as you sing.

begin here:

Choose someone to be Mr. Monday.
He may select his own instrument and make up a special part.
Here is how the class asks him to play.

Hey there Mis - ter Mon - day,   Play for   me,   play   for   me.

Hey there Mis - ter   Mon - day,   Play so   fine   for   me.

Mr. Monday plays his part.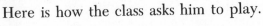

Someone else plays the bell accompaniment.

Now choose someone to be Mr. Tuesday.
He may make up a special part to play on another instrument.
The class sings, "Hey there, Mister Tuesday. . ."

Mr. Tuesday plays his part.

Someone else plays the bell accompaniment.

Can you play and sing about each day of the week?

Old Brass Wagon

Midwestern Play-Party Game

1. Cir - cle to the left, Old Brass Wag - on,

Cir - cle to the left, Old Brass Wag - on,

Cir - cle to the left, Old Brass Wag - on,

You're the one, my dar - ling.

2. Swing, oh, swing, Old Brass Wagon, *(3 times)*
   You're the one, my darling.

3. Skipping all around, Old Brass Wagon, *(3 times)*
   You're the one, my darling.

Percussion Melee

by Rudolph Ganz

Do you hear instruments that sound like the ones
you play in class? Which ones can you name?

The Cat

Music by Ronald Lo Presti
Words by B.A.

Sounds can be soft.

Sounds suddenly can become **loud**.

p
Why - a - mese are Si - a - mese so sly - a - mese?

pp   *ff*
They sneak,   and creep,   then sud - den - ly   they leap!

Use loud and soft sounds as you sing this song.
Where will you sing softly? Loudly?

The Cuckoo

German Folk Song

Which parts of this song will you sing loudly?
Which parts will you sing softly?

1. Cuck-oo!   Cuck-oo!   Don't try to   hide from me;
2. Cuck-oo!   Cuck-oo!   It's such an   eas-y   song;

Cuck-oo!   Cuck-oo!   I   see you   in the   tree.
Cuck-oo!   Cuck-oo!   It's hard to   get it   wrong.

Play the "cuckoo" echo on the bells.
Which of these bells will you play?

5

THE SCHOOL BUS

When is it very quiet inside the school bus?

When does it become loud inside the school bus?

When does it become very loud inside the school bus?

This is a picture of very quiet becoming loud.

This is a picture of very loud becoming quiet.

Show how the school bus sounds coming to school.
Show how it sounds going away from school.

6

Down by the Station

Traditional Southern Song

Down by the sta - tion ear - ly in the morn - ing,

See the lit - tle puf - fer - bil - lies all in a row.

See the en - gine driv - er pull the lit - tle han - dle.

Choo! Choo! Toot! Toot! Off they go!

Make up an **introduction** for your song that sounds like this:

Make up a **coda** for your song that sounds like this:

What instruments will you use?

Rhythm in Our World

There is rhythm in the sounds of your feet,

There is rhythm in the words that you speak.

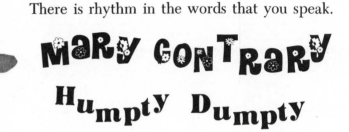

MARY CONTRARY

Humpty Dumpty

There is rhythm in the rooms of your home,

There is rhythm when
you're outside alone.

Inside, outside, all around I've found
Rhythms have many a wondrous sound!

8

Rhythm in Our Classroom

Can you clap a steady beat?

♩   ♩   ♩   ♩

Can you clap, pat your leg, and keep a steady beat?

Let's Call the Roll

Can you accompany the roll call with a steady beat?

Who is   here in   school to- day?

Call the roll   just this way.

My   name is Bob-   by,

Bob-   by   Mar-   tin.

9

I Should Like to Go to Texas

Traditional

I should like to go to Tex - as,

Come and take a ride with me.

I should like to ride a bron - co,

I can ride one, watch and see.

10

Use your finger and slide across the lines as you sing.

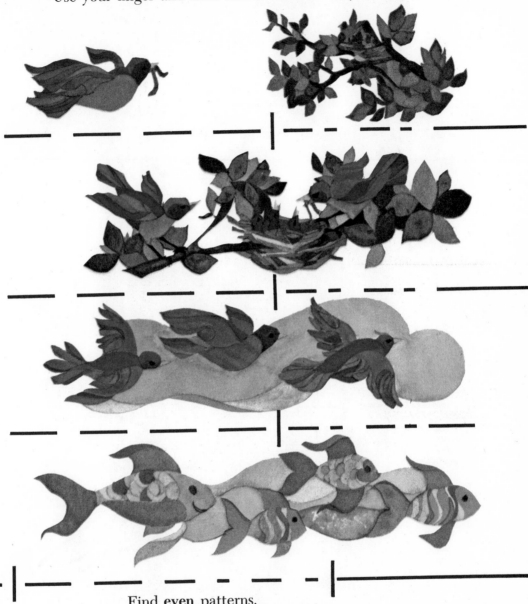

Find **even** patterns.
Find **uneven** patterns.
How many **phrases** can you find?
Which phrases are exactly the same?
Which phrase is almost the same?
Which phrase is different?

13

Syncopated Clock

by Leroy Anderson

This is a mixed-up clock!
Can you see what is wrong with it?

Can you hear what is wrong with it?
Does the clock always keep a steady beat?

——— — — — — —

Raise your hand when the clock does this:

——— — — — —   or   — — — —

Play these instruments with the sounds of
this mixed-up clock on the recording.

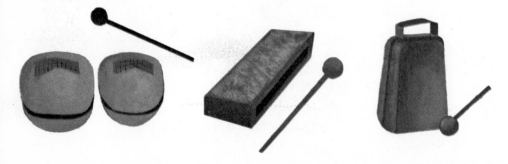

The Well

by B.A.

Highly-oh-up!
I'll walk and hop,
When I reach the sun,
That's where I'll stop!

Down
a
deep
well
a
grasshopper
fell.

Middley-oh-up!
I'll walk and hop,
When I reach the sun,
That's where I'll stop!

Lowly-oh-up!
I'll walk and hop,
When I reach the sun,
That's where I'll stop!

Find instruments to help tell this story.
Find an instrument that will give the feeling
   of a sudden fall.
Find instruments that sound low, in the middle, and high.

A Number Song

Find these bells.
Put them in a row.
Play the bells from low to high, then from high to low.
Did the melody move by steps or skips?

Chant the words.
Sing the words as you play the bells.

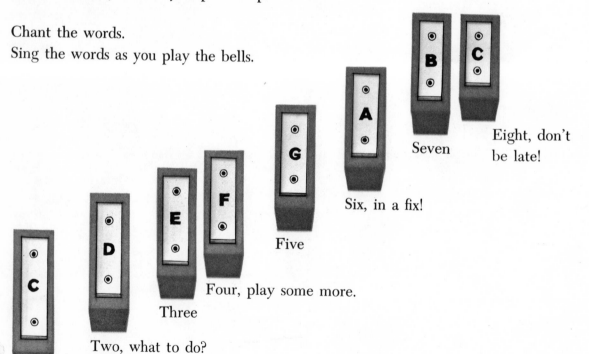

One

Two, what to do?

Three

Four, play some more.

Five

Six, in a fix!

Seven

Eight, don't
be late!

See Saw

by Evelyn Beyer

Arrange your bells in this order:

Make up a melody to match the words of this poem.
Write the numbers of the bells you played.
The numbers will help you remember your melody.
Did your melody move by steps or skips?

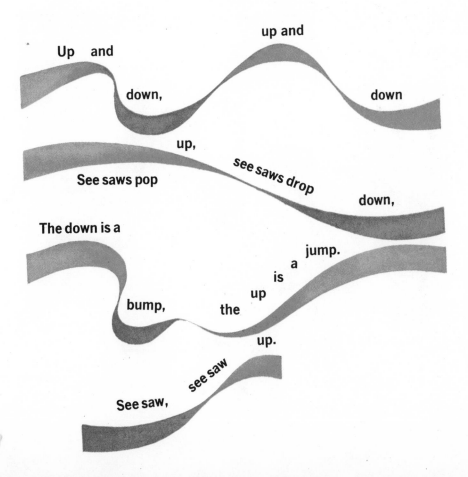

Play and sing Melodies

Go to Sleep

Spanish Folk Song

Here are two songs to learn by reading the numbers.
Play them on the bells. Sing the numbers. Sing the words.

You will need these bells: F G A B♭ C
                                   1 2 3 4 5

my
5

sleep
3

to
2

Go
1

by,
5

ba -
3

tle
2

lit -
1

and
5

eyes
3

your
2

Close
1

do
3

not
2

cry.
1

18

Oliver Twist

Traditional

Which of these bells will you play?

D	E	F#	G	A	B	C#	D
1	2	3	4	5	6	7	8(1)

O - li- ver   can't   do
5   5   5   5   5

Twist,   you   this,   so
3   3   3   3

of
6

what's   the   use   try -
5   5   5   5

ing?
3

Pictures of melodies can be written on a **staff** with notes.
The notes show patterns that

step   skip   stay the same

Which staff shows the picture of "Go to Sleep"?
Which staff shows the picture of "Oliver Twist"?

Hoot Owl Song

Chippewa Folk Song

The song says, "I'm afraid of the big white owl."
Look at the music.
When does the melody stay the same?
Can you find a place where it moves by skips? By steps?

1. Ku - ku - ku' u ning - o - sa,
2. Wa - bi - ku - ku ning - o - sa,

Ku - ku - ku' u ning - o - sa, ning - o - sa,
Wa - bi - ku - ku ning - o - sa, ning - o - sa,

Ku - ku - ku___ ning - o - sa.
Wa - bi - ku - ku ning - o - sa.

Accompany the song with a steady beat on a drum.

20

I'll Sing You a Song

Music by Paul Kapp
Traditional Words

I'll sing you a song, though not ver - y long,

Yet I think it's as pret - ty as an - y; ____

Put your hand in your purse, you'll nev - er do worse,

And give the poor sing - er a pen - ny. ____

21

Listen for Many Sounds

Sit quietly in your room.
What sounds do you hear?
Do you hear more than one sound at the same time?

Listen to Music

Court Dances of Medieval France

How many different sounds do you hear?
As you listen, point to the picture that matches the music.

Listen to other music.
Make your own picture.

Rain Song

Music by Irving Lowens
Words Anonymous

Listen to the recording of this song.
Listen to the voices.
Do you also hear some instruments?
The instruments play an accompaniment.

The rain sings a song all night long.

All through the dark I hear it sing - ing;

Sing - ing its song all night long. ____

How did the high accompaniment move?
Can you play it on the bells?
Play it while the class sings.

Suite for Toy Piano

Fifth Piece

by John Cage

Do all pianos look alike? Do they sound alike?
Does a toy piano sound like a real piano?
Make up a piece on a toy piano.

Hear my toy pi - a - no,

Hear it as I play.

Play a tune

Hear my toy pi - a - no,

Play a tune

Hear it as I play.

Play a tune

Now listen to the piece by John Cage written especially for a toy piano.

America

Music attributed to Henry Carey
Words by Samuel F. Smith

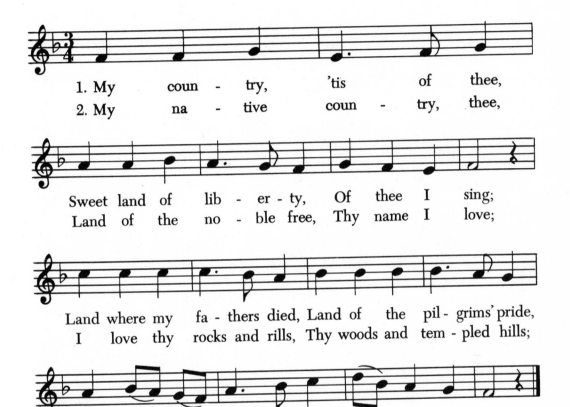

1. My coun - try, 'tis of thee,
2. My na - tive coun - try, thee,

Sweet land of lib - er - ty, Of thee I sing;
Land of the no - ble free, Thy name I love;

Land where my fa - thers died, Land of the pil - grims' pride,
I love thy rocks and rills, Thy woods and tem - pled hills;

From ev - ery __ moun - tain - side Let __ free - dom ring.
My heart __ with __ rap - ture thrills Like __ that a - bove.

Can you find rhythm patterns in music?
Find this uneven pattern.

'tis of thee

Find this even pattern.

My coun - try

25

Sounds of Rhythm

Can you . . . .

Clap beats?

Hear rhythm in music?

Hear rhythm in words?

Draw a picture of rhythm?

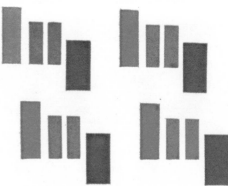

Play rhythm patterns?

Dance a rhythm pattern?

Describe it with words?

Walk in rhythm?

SENDING SOUNDS

Let's send long and short sounds.
Stand facing a friend with the palms
 of your hands held up.
Your friend holds his hands still while you
 send him sounds.
Send these sounds with your right hand.

Let your partner send you short sounds
 with his right hand.

Can you and your partner send sounds to each other
 at the same time?

You send

Your partner sends

Scotland's Burning

Traditional Round

Play these bells as you sing.

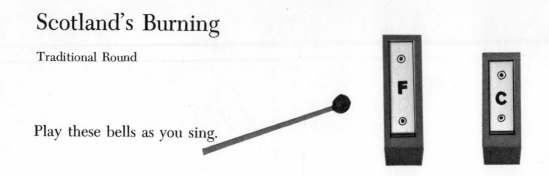

Play the bells in one of these rhythm patterns.

In which pattern will the notes sound with the beat?
In which pattern will the notes sound two to a beat?

Scot-land's burn-ing, Scot-land's burn-ing, Look out, look out.

Fire, fire, fire, fire, Pour on wa-ter, pour on wa-ter!

Which of your accompaniments make the song
   seem more exciting? Why?
Find an instrument to play which expresses
   the excitement of "Fire! Fire!"

Mary Mack

Melody by Ella Jenkins
First verse adapted by Ella Jenkins
Additional verses traditional

Ma- ry Mack, dressed in black, sil - ver but- tons down her back.

Hi - o!   Hi - o!   Hi - o! Hi - o!   Hi - o!

2. Asked her mother for fifteen cents to
See the elephants jump the fence.
Refrain

3. Jumped so high, they touched the sky,
Never came back 'til the fourth of July.
Refrain

Two of the sounds which you sing are long sounds.
They are shown with notes that look like this:

Can you find these long notes in the music?
Can you show the long sounds in the way you move?

Hi - O!   Hi - O!

Jingle at the Windows

Singing Game

Listen to the music.
Follow the notes with a "sliding" finger as you listen.
Does 𝅗𝅥 sound longer or shorter than ♩ ?

Pass one win - dow, ti - de - o,

Pass two win - dows, ti - de - o,

Pass three win - dows, ti - de - o,

Jin - gle at the win - dows, ti - de - o.

Ti - de - o, ti - de - o,

Jin - gle at the win - dows, ti - de - o.

Join into the Game

Additional words and music adaptation
by Paul Campbell (The Weavers)

Swinging

C   G7   C

Let ev - ery - one clap hands like me, *(clap, clap)*

C   G7   C

Let ev - ery - one clap hands like me. *(clap, clap)*

Refrain

C   C7   F

Come on and join in - to the game; _____

G7   G7   C

You'll find that it's al - ways the same. *(clap, clap)*

Can you make up verses for instruments?

2. Let everyone play bells like me.

3. Let everyone play drums like me.

4. Let everyone play sticks like me.

Circle Around

German Folk Dance
Words by Margaret Lowrey

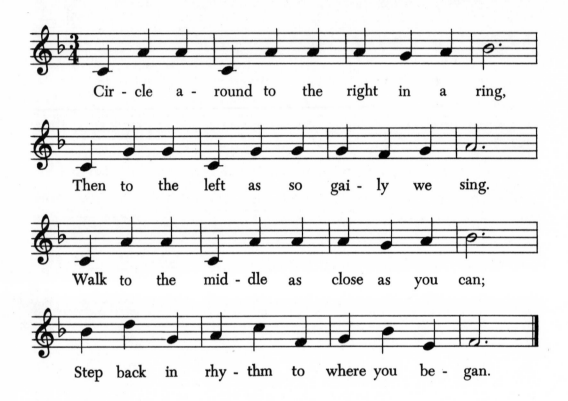

Cir - cle a - round to   the   right in   a   ring,

Then to the left as so gai - ly we sing.

Walk to the mid - dle as close as you can;

Step back in rhy - thm to where you be - gan.

Tap the beat as you listen to the music.
Which picture shows the way the beats move?

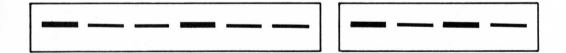

Listen again to "Jingle at the Windows" and tap the beat.
Which picture shows the way the beats move in that song?

The Little Car

by Norman Cazden

There was a lit-tle car. ___ The cut-est lit-tle car, ___

The cut-est lit-tle car you ev-er did see,

And the car was on the wheels,

And the wheels were on the ground,

And the en-gine in the car ___ made the wheels go round.

Choose an instrument to make the sound of the wheels turning.
Did you make an even or uneven pattern?
Draw a picture of the pattern you made.

Find these short and long notes in the music: ♪ | ♩ ♪ ♩ ♪ | ♩.

Is this rhythm pattern even or uneven?

Johnny Schmoker

Pennsylvania Dutch Folk Song

1. John - ny Schmo - ker, John - ny Schmo - ker,

Can you sing, _____ can you play? _____

I can play up - on my vi - o - lin.

Fid - dle did - dle dee, so sings my vi - o - lin.

2. Johnny Schmoker, Johnny Schmoker,
   Can you sing, can you play?
   I can play upon my clarinet.
   Doodle doodle doo, so sings my clarinet.

3. Johnny Schmoker, Johnny Schmoker,
   Can you sing, can you play?
   I can play upon my silver flute.
   Tootle tootle toot, so sings my silver flute.

34

The Eagle Dance

Southwest Indian Dance

Part 1

Part 2

Part 3

Can you imagine how the dancers might move
when the drum changes rhythm?

Lone Star Trail

American Cowboy Song

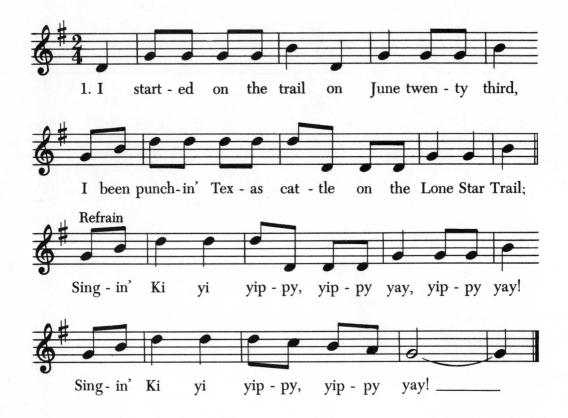

1. I start - ed on the trail on June twen - ty third,

I been punch-in' Tex - as cat - tle on the Lone Star Trail;

Refrain

Sing - in' Ki yi yip - py, yip - py yay, yip - py yay!

Sing - in' Ki yi yip - py, yip - py yay! _____

2. I get up in the morn before the daylight,
   And before I go to sleep the moon is shining bright.
   Refrain

3. It's bacon and it's beans almost every day,
   But I wouldn't mind a change if it was prairie hay.
   Refrain

THE CATTLE DRIVE

Cowboys hear many different sounds when they are on the trail.
See if you can follow the trail of the cattle drive.
Tap these rhythm patterns and chant the words.

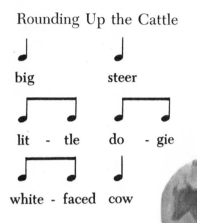

Rounding Up the Cattle

big   steer

lit - tle   do - gie

white - faced cow

On the Drive

chuck   wag - on

jan - gling spurs

whoa

At the Shipping Yard

choo   choo

toot!

ding - ding, ding - ding!

Which of these rhythm patterns are the same?
Choose instruments to help you tell this story.
Play any three rhythm patterns to accompany the class
   as it sings "Lone Star Trail."

Yankee Doodle

Traditional American Song

Fa-ther and I went down to camp,

A - long with Cap - tain Good - ing,

And there we met the men and boys,

As thick as hast - y pud - ding.

Refrain

Yan - kee Doo - dle, keep it up,

Yan - kee Doo - dle dan - dy,

Mind the mu - sic and the step,

And with the girls be hand - y.

Can you find sounds to describe Yankee Doodle going to camp?
Use instruments or your own body sounds.
Will Yankee Doodle be riding his horse?

Playing a drum?

Walking?

Did he whistle while he walked?

What other sounds did he make?
Use your sounds to accompany the song.

39

Call to Colors

A very special call is played when the flag is raised.
Here are the notes of this bugle call.
Can you see and hear when the sounds go up? When they go down?

The Star-Spangled Banner

Composer Unknown
Words by Francis Scott Key

Our national anthem is a song which honors our country.
We can sing this song or listen to it being played.

Listen to a band playing our national anthem.
What instruments do you hear?

Semper Fidelis

by John Philip Sousa

Listen to this famous march.
Why does the music make your toes want to tap?
Do you know what instruments play in a band?
Make up movements to this march.

Here Rover!

Which rhythm would you choose to accompany this poem?

Here Rov-er, Here Rov-er

Here Rov-er, Rov-er, Here Rov-er, Rov-er

I had a little dog, his name was Rover,
When he died, he died all over.

I had a little dog, his name was Trot,
He held up his tail all tied in a knot.

Which rhythm would you choose to accompany this poem?

Oh, where, oh, where has my little dog gone,
Oh, where, oh, where can he be?
With his tail cut short and his ears cut long,
Oh, where, oh, where can he be?

41

El coquí (The Frog)

Puerto Rican Folk Song

Sing this song in English.
Then learn to sing it in Spanish.
Listen to the recording to learn the Spanish words.

With a swinging motion

El co - quí, el co - quí so en - chants me;
El co - quí, el co - quí, a mi me en can - ta,

El co - quí sings his song all night long.
Es tan lin - do el can - tar del co - quí;

Ev - ery night when I lie on my pil - low,
Por las noch - es al ir a a - cost - ar - me,

With his sing - ing he lulls me to sleep. ___
Me a - dor - me - ce can - tan - do a - sí. ___

42

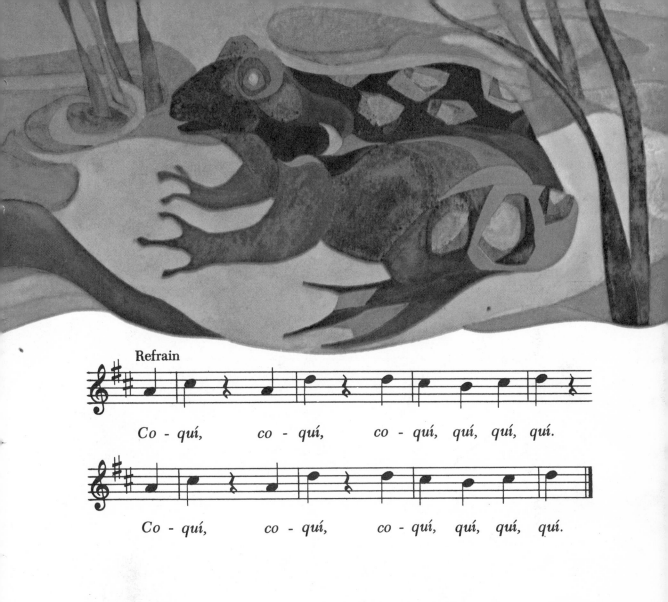

Refrain

Co - quí,   co - quí,   co - quí, quí, quí, quí.

Co - quí,   co - quí,   co - quí, quí, quí, quí.

Slide your finger under the notes of the refrain as you
   listen to the recording.

Listen carefully to the singers.

Notice that they are silent each time you come to this sign ⸮

It is called a **rest**.

Can you tap this pattern? Tap the **notes**.

Be silent during the **rests**.

43

Halloween

Words and Music
by Lynn Olson

You should know it's the time of year

When the witch - es and ghosts ap - pear.

They come at night when there's no more light;

Hal - low - een is al - most here.

If you look ver - y care - ful - ly,

There's a gob - lin be - hind that tree.

But I must say, don't you run a - way,

'Cause it might be me!

Strange Halloween

Words and Music
by Eunice Boardman

Hal - low - een! Strange things seen! Ghosts may walk,

Skel - e - tons talk on Hal - low - een! Hal - low - een!

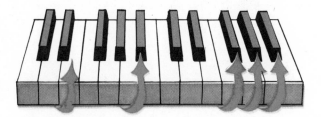

Play the keys that are marked.

Find the melody for the word "Halloween" on the
low part of the piano.

Play the melody for "Ghosts may walk" on the
high tones of the piano.

I'm Not Scared

by B.A.

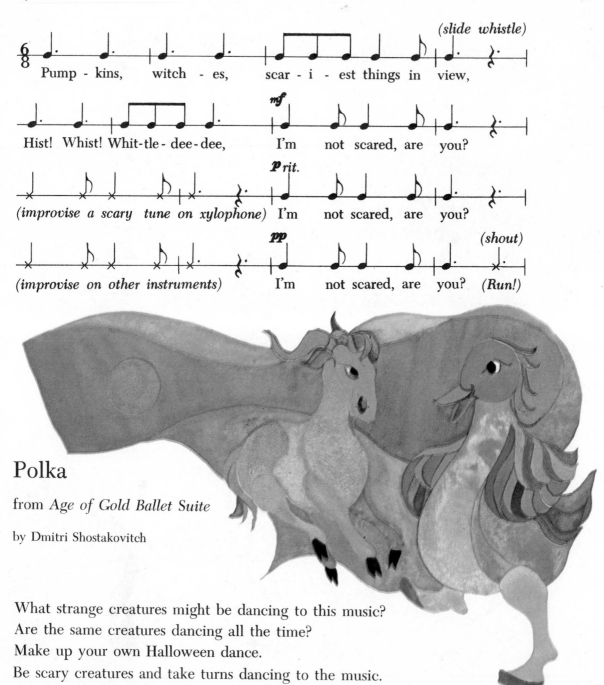

(slide whistle)

Pump - kins, witch - es, scar - i - est things in view,

Hist! Whist! Whit-tle-dee-dee, I'm not scared, are you?

(improvise a scary tune on xylophone) I'm not scared, are you?

(improvise on other instruments) I'm not scared, are you? *(Run!)*

(shout)

Polka

from *Age of Gold Ballet Suite*

by Dmitri Shostakovitch

What strange creatures might be dancing to this music?
Are the same creatures dancing all the time?
Make up your own Halloween dance.
Be scary creatures and take turns dancing to the music.

Ngoye

African Folk Song

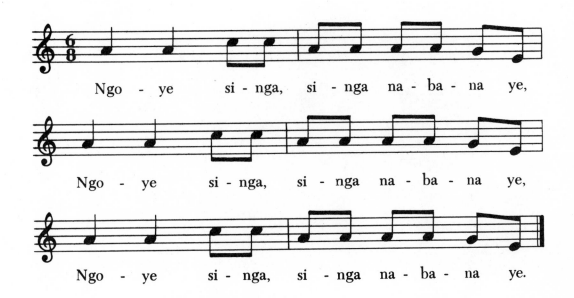

Ngo - ye si - nga, si - nga na - ba - na ye,

Ngo - ye si - nga, si - nga na - ba - na ye,

Ngo - ye si - nga, si - nga na - ba - na ye.

Listen to the recording. Find these patterns.
Play the patterns on instruments.

Gretel, Pastetel

German Folk Song

C   C   F   C

1. Gret - el, Pas - tet - el, oh where is your goose?
2. Gret - el, Pas - tet - el, oh where is your hen?
3. Gret - el, Pas - tet - el, oh where is your cow?

F   C   G7   C

She sits in the wa - ter, oh who turned her loose?
She sits on her nest and lays eggs when she can.
She stays in her stall but I can't milk her now.

This song moves in threes. Can you clap HEAVY light light as you sing?

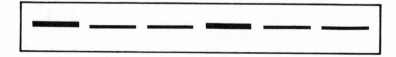

48

Play this part of "Gretel, Pastetel" on the bells.

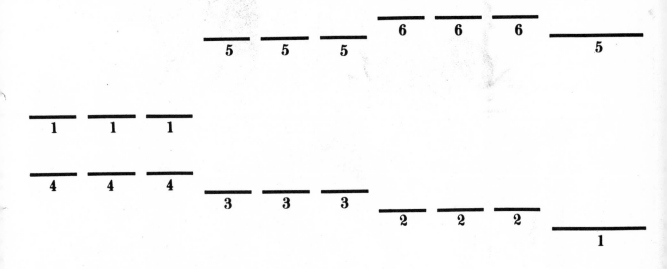

Take away one beat from each bell's sounds.
The song now moves in twos.
Sing it this new way with numbers.

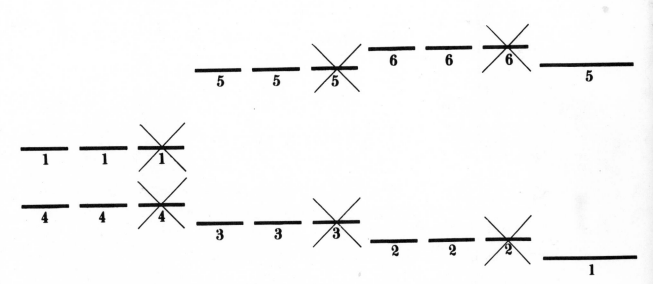

What familiar song have you discovered?

Variations on "Ah, vous dirai-je maman"
Theme and Variations 4, 5, 8, 12

by Wolfgang Amadeus Mozart

How many different ways can you get from one place to another?

Melodies can get from one place to another in different
 ways too!

Listen to this music.
How does it change each time the melody is repeated?
Can you dance the different ways the music moves?

Arranged and conducted
by Gershon Kingsley
on the Moog Synthesizer

Do you hear anything in this music you've heard before?
What is different?

Pawpaw Patch

American Singing Game

This is a dancing song.
Sing the song and dance as you sing.

1. Where, O where is pret - ty lit - tle El - lie,

Where, O where is pret - ty lit - tle El - lie,

Where, O where is pret - ty lit - tle El - lie?

'Way down yon - der in the paw - paw patch.

2. Pickin' up pawpaws, puttin' em in a basket, *(3 times)*
'Way down yonder in the pawpaw patch.

3. Here she comes, let's all go with her, *(3 times)*
'Way down yonder in the pawpaw patch.

Sounds of Melody

Can you . . .

Sing a melody?

Describe a melody with words?

Play a melody?

Hear a melody?

Make up your own melody?

Draw a melody's shape?

Dance a melody?

Dickery Dickery Dare

Traditional

Dickery dickery dare
The pig flew up in the air!
The man in brown
Soon brought him down.
Dickery dickery dare!

Make up a melody you can sing.
Make your melody match the words of the poem.
Use some of these bells.

Little Bo-Peep

Music by J. W. Elliott
Words from Mother Goose

You can learn to sing a melody by listening.
As you listen, show the shape of the melody with your hands.
Draw its shape on the chalkboard.

1. Lit - tle Bo - Peep has lost her sheep,

And can't tell where____ to find them;

Leave them a - lone, and they'll come home,

Wag- ging their tails ___ be - hind them.

2. Little Bo-Peep fell fast asleep,
   And dreamed she heard them bleating;
   When she awoke, 'twas all a joke,
   For they were still a-fleeting.

3. Then up she took her little crook,
   Determined for to find them;
   What was her joy to see them nigh,
   Wagging their tails behind them.

Children's Symphony

Second Movement

by Harl McDonald

A composer used the melody of "Little Bo-Peep" in his
  composition for **orchestra.**
Does the melody sound the same as the melody you sang?
Can you hear a new melody?
Do you hear the "Little Bo-Peep" melody again?

Plan a dance for this composition.
Can you show the two melodies as you dance?

Old Roger Is Dead

Traditional

Can you learn to play and sing this song?
Look at the notes on the staff.
Look at the numbers below the staff.
The C bell will be 1.
Can you find the other bells you will need?
When you know the song, act out the words as you sing.

1. Old Rog - er is dead, and gone to his grave.
   5   8   8   8   5   5   3   3   3   1

Ha, ha, gone to his grave.
8   5   5   6   7   8

2. They planted an apple tree over his head,
   Ha, ha, over his head.

3. The apples were ripe and ready to drop,
   Ha, ha, ready to drop.

4. There came an east wind a-blowing them off,
   Ha, ha, blowing them off.

5. There came an old woman a-picking them up,
   Ha, ha, picking them up.

6. Old Roger jumped up and gave her a knock,
   Ha, ha, gave her a knock.

7. Which made the old woman go hippity hop,
   Ha, ha, hippity hop.

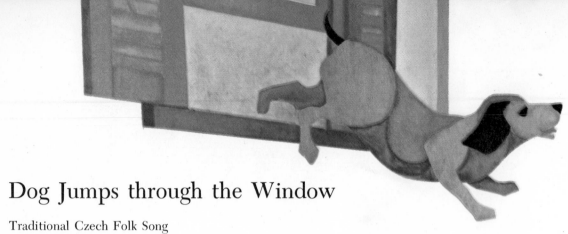

Dog Jumps through the Window

Traditional Czech Folk Song
Translation by Vilem Tausky

Dog jumps through the   win - dow,   Puss   hides   too;
1   2   3   4   5   5   6   6   5

If   it   does - n't   rain,   We'll   keep   dry   too.
4   4   4   4   3   3   2   2   1

Can you learn to sing this melody by looking at the notes
   and singing the numbers?
Play the melody on these bells.

The D bell will be 1.

58

An Event for 3 Performers

Have you ever seen a timer that looks like this?
Describe the timer with music.

Player 1 can make the sound of sand.

player 1

player 2   player 3

Idea 1   Players 2 and 3 can play the
high and low bells to describe how
the sand changes from high to low.

or

Idea 2   Player 2 can describe how much sand
is in the low part by playing many or
few sounds.

Player 3 can describe how much sand
is in the high part by playing many or
few sounds.

Can you use Ideas 1 and 2 at the same time
   to describe the timer?
Can all performers play their parts at the same time?
Give your event a name.
Perform it for your classmates.

Barnyard Song

Kentucky Mountain Folk Song

Look at the music.
Which animal sound goes up?
Which goes down?
Which stays the same?
Listen to the recording. Were you right?

1. I had a cat and the cat pleased me,
2. I had a hen and the hen pleased me,
3. I had a duck and the duck pleased me,

I fed my cat by yon - der tree;
I fed my hen by yon - der tree;
I fed my duck by yon - der tree;

Sing this melody after verse 1.

D.S.

Cat goes fid - dle - i - fee.____

60

Sing this melody after verse 2.

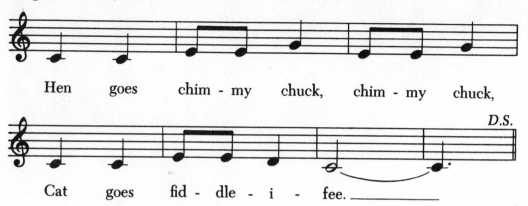

Hen   goes   chim - my   chuck,   chim - my   chuck,

D.S.

Cat   goes   fid - dle - i - fee. _____

Sing this melody after verse 3.

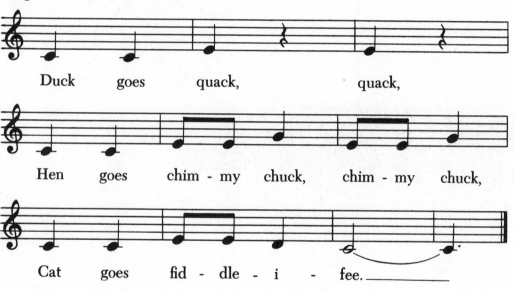

Duck   goes   quack,   quack,

Hen   goes   chim - my   chuck,   chim - my   chuck,

Cat   goes   fid - dle - i - fee. _____

Play the sounds of each animal. Use these bells.

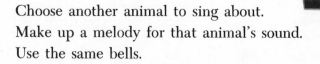

Choose another animal to sing about.
Make up a melody for that animal's sound.
Use the same bells.

Skip to My Lou

American Singing Game

This is a singing dance of long ago.
Your grandfather may know it.
Dance and clap as you sing.

Verse

1. Lost my part - ner, what will I do?

Lost my part - ner, what will I do?

Lost my part - ner, what will I do?

Skip to my Lou, my dar - ling.

Refrain

Skip, skip, skip to my Lou,

Skip, skip, skip to my Lou,

Skip, skip, skip to my Lou,

Skip to my Lou, my dar - ling.

2. I'll get another one, pretty as you, *(3 times)*
   Skip to my Lou, my darling.
   Refrain

3. Little red wagon, painted blue, *(3 times)*
   Skip to my Lou, my darling.
   Refrain

4. Fly in the sugar bowl, shoo, fly, shoo, *(3 times)*
   Skip to my Lou, my darling.
   Refrain

Carrousel

Swedish Play Song

Do you know what a carrousel is?
Look at the painting on page 172 to help you decide.
Have you ever ridden on a carrousel?
How did the ponies move?
Listen to the music.
Does it move the same way the ponies did?
Show the shape of the melody with your hands.

1. How we love to ride the car - rou - sel,
2. While we're rid - ing on the car - rou - sel,

Round and round ad - vanc - ing, on our po - nies pranc - ing.
Up and down we're bounc - ing, in the sad - dle jounc - ing.

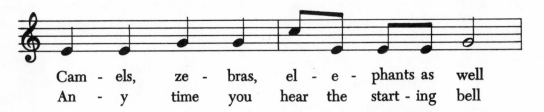

Cam - els, ze - bras, el - e - phants as well
An - y time you hear the start - ing bell

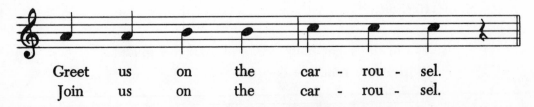

Greet us on the car - rou - sel.
Join us on the car - rou - sel.

Refrain

Ha, ha, ha! Hap - py are we,

An - der - son and Hen - der - son and Lund - strom and me.

Play a melody pattern that goes ^{up} and _{down} by **skips** as you sing the verse.

C G C G

Play a melody pattern that goes ^{up} by **steps** as you sing the refrain.

G G A A B B C C

Bye'm Bye

Texas Folk Game

Can you sing and play these patterns from the song?

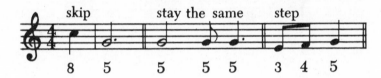

Can you sing the whole song?

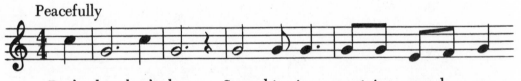

Bye'm bye, bye'm bye, Stars shin - ing, count - ing, num - ber one,

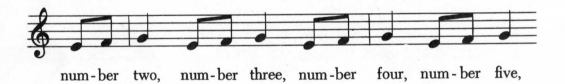

num - ber two, num - ber three, num - ber four, num - ber five,

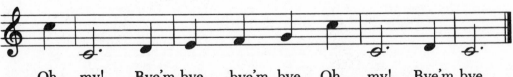

Oh my! Bye'm bye, bye'm bye, Oh my! Bye'm bye.

66

There Was a Crooked Man

Traditional Melody
Words from Mother Goose

Play this crooked melody.

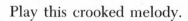
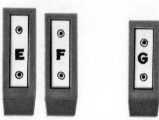

Does it step or skip?
Which bells will you play?

Can you find a crooked melody that moves by steps?

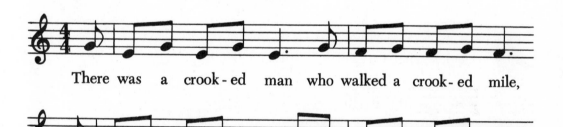

There was a crook-ed man who walked a crook-ed mile,

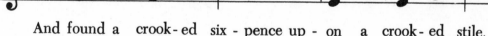

And found a crook-ed six-pence up-on a crook-ed stile.

He bought a crook-ed cat that caught a crook-ed mouse,

And they all lived to-geth-er in a lit-tle crook-ed house.

Hold On!

Spiritual

This song is a Black spiritual. Listen to the music.
Can you decide what the word "spiritual" means?

As you listen, clap this rhythm.

If you want to get to heav-en I'll tell you how,

Just keep your hand on the gos-pel plow. __

68

Keep your hand on the plow, — hold on, hold on.

If that plow stays in your hand,

Land you straight in the prom - ised land. —

Keep your hand on the plow, — hold on, hold on.

Hold on, ———— hold on. ————

Keep — your hand on the plow, — hold on, hold on.

Listen to the "Tell Tale Singers" sing "Hold On!"
What differences do you notice?
Is the melody exactly the same as the melody you learned?
What do you notice about the accompaniment?

Kokoleoko

(The Rooster's Call)

Folk Song from Liberia

How many patterns can you find that use these tones?
Do they step or skip?

Play the pattern on the bells as you sing.

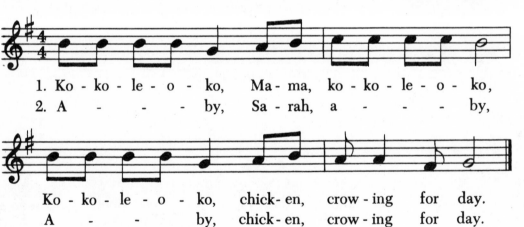

1. Ko - ko - le - o - ko, Ma - ma, ko - ko - le - o - ko,
2. A - - by, Sa - rah, a - - by,

Ko - ko - le - o - ko, chick - en, crow - ing for day.
A - - by, chick - en, crow - ing for day.

3. One more round, Te-te, one more round,
   One more round, chicken, crowing for day.

4. Take your time, baby, take your time,
   Take your time, chicken, crowing for day.

Grace

Chinese Folk Tune
Words by T. C. Chao
Translation by Bliss Wiant

Ne'er for - get God's dai - ly ___ care:

Health and food ___ and ___ clothes to wear.

Free - ly we these gifts re - ceive.

May we not ___ his ___ spir - it grieve.

Can you say "thank you" in many different languages?

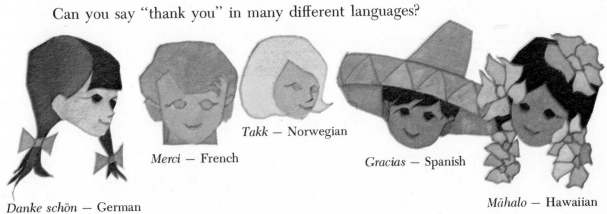

Merci — French

Takk — Norwegian

Gracias — Spanish

Danke schön — German

Māhalo — Hawaiian

Use these words in a thank-you chant.

Over the River and through the Wood

Traditional Tune
Words by Lydia Maria Child

Listen to the recording of this song.
Listen for the introduction played by the **French horn.**
Listen for the **oboe** at the end of the first verse.

Plan an accompaniment for this song.
Choose an instrument that sounds like horses galloping along.
Decide on a rhythm pattern.
Will it be even or uneven?

Play a rhythm pattern with jingle bells while you sing the
    second verse.

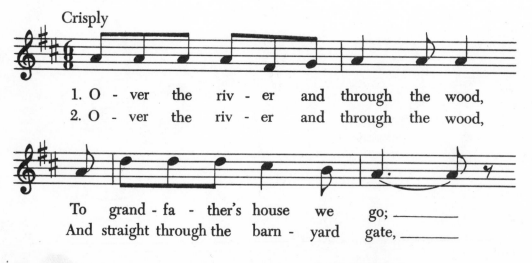

Crisply

1. O - ver the riv - er and through the wood,
2. O - ver the riv - er and through the wood,

To grand - fa - ther's house we go; _____
And straight through the barn - yard gate, _____

The horse knows the way to car - ry the sleigh
We seem __ to go ex - treme - ly slow,

Through the white and drift - ed snow. _____
It __ is so hard to wait! _____

O - ver the riv - er and through the wood,
O - ver the riv - er and through the wood,

Oh, how the wind does blow! _____
Now grand-moth-er's cap I spy! _____

It stings the toes and bites the nose
Hur - rah for the fun! Is the pud - ding done?

As o - ver the ground we go. _____
Hur - rah for the pump - kin pie! _____

Lavender's Blue

English Folk Song

1. Lav - en - der's blue, dil - ly, dil - ly, lav - en - der's green,
2. Call up your men, dil - ly, dil - ly, set them to work,

When I am King, dil - ly, dil - ly, you shall be Queen;
Some with a rake, dil - ly, dil - ly, some with a fork;

Who told you so? dil - ly, dil - ly, who told you so?
Some to make hay, dil - ly, dil - ly, some to thresh corn,

'Twas mine own heart, dil - ly, dil - ly, that told me so.
While you and I, dil - ly, dil - ly, keep our - selves warm.

Can you put these bells in order from low to high?

Play the melody for "'Twas mine own heart,
    dilly, dilly" on the bells.
How did it move?
The pattern you played is called a **scale.**

Can you play another scale on the piano?
Start here:

You will need to play both black and white keys.

How many black keys will you need to play the scale?

Sing! Sing! Sing!

Brazilian Folk Game

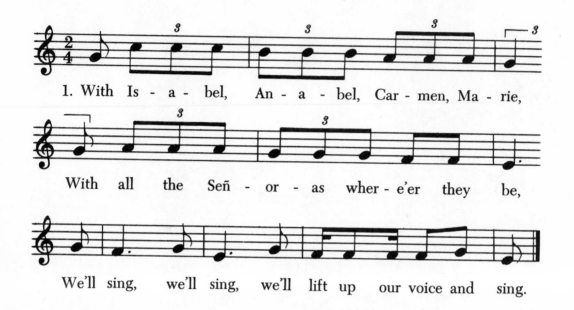

1. With Is - a - bel, An - a - bel, Car - men, Ma - rie,

With all the Señ - or - as wher - e'er they be,

We'll sing, we'll sing, we'll lift up our voice and sing.

2. With rich man and poor man and beggar and thief,
   With doctor and lawyer and Indian chief,
   We'll sing, we'll sing, we'll lift up our voice and sing.

3. In Uruguay, Paraguay, Chile, Peru,
   Brazil, Venezuela, Bolivia, too,
   We'll sing, we'll sing, we'll lift up our voice and sing.

While the class sings the first two phrases, play a pattern on the bells that moves down the scale by steps.

While the class sings the third phrase, play a pattern that moves by skips.

The Owl and the Pussycat

Poem by Edward Lear
Music by Igor Stravinsky

Listen to the poem as it is read.
A composer wrote music for this poem.
Follow the pictures and words as the poem is sung.

you are

you are

What a beautiful pussy you are

his nose

his nose

With a ring at the end of his nose.

78

the moon

the moon

*And they danced by
the light of the moon. . . .*

How did the music express the rocking movement of the boat?
Did the piano ever play the melody?

The Frogs

Traditional Round

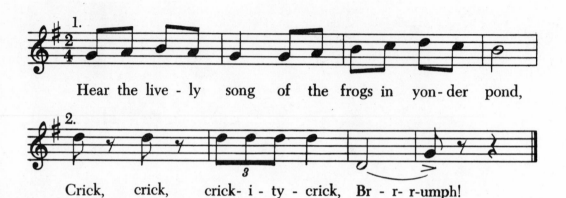

Hear the live - ly   song   of   the   frogs   in   yon-der   pond,

Crick,   crick,   crick- i - ty - crick, Br - r- r-umph!

What is the longest sound the frogs make?
What is the shortest sound?
Find an instrument that can sound like:

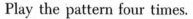

Br - r - r - ump!

and one that can sound like:

Crick,   crick,   crick - i -   ty -   crick,

Add this accompaniment to your song.
Play the pattern four times.

Can you find this melody in the song?

Hanukah

Jewish Folk Song

Lively

1. Ha - nu - kah, Ha - nu - kah, Fes - ti - val of Lights;
2. Ha - nu - kah, Ha - nu - kah, What a mer - ry time;

Can - dles glow in a row, Sev - en days, eight nights.
Cakes to eat, what a treat, See the fac - es shine!

Ha - nu - kah, Ha - nu - kah, Make your drey - dls spin
Ha - nu - kah, Ha - nu - kah, Sing and dance this way:

Round and round, round and round, Ev - ery - one join in!
Round and round, round and round, Hap - py hol - i - day!

All Night, All Day

Spiritual

All night,

all day,

Quietly

Refrain

All night, all _____ day,

An - gels watch - ing o - ver me, my Lord, __

All night, all _____ day,

Fine

An - gels watch - ing o - ver me. _____

82

Angels watching over me...

Now I lay me down to sleep,

Pray the Lord...

Verse

1. Now I lay me down __ to sleep,
2. If I die be - fore __ I wake,

An - gels watch - ing o - ver me, my Lord, __

Pray the Lord my soul __ to keep,
Pray the Lord my soul __ to take.

D.C. al Fine

An - gels watch - ing o - ver me. _____

83

Wind through the Olive Trees

Traditional Carol

1. Wind through the ol - ive trees Soft - ly did blow,

Round lit - tle Beth - le - hem, Long, long a - go.

2. Sheep on the hillside lay
   Whiter than snow,
   Shepherds were watching them,
   Long, long ago.

3. Then from the starry skies
   Angels bent low,
   Singing their songs of joy,
   Long, long ago.

4. For in a manger bed
   Long, long ago,
   Christ came to Bethlehem,
   Long, long ago.

Silent Night

Music by Franz Gruber
Words translated by
John F. Young from
the German by Joseph Mohr

Si - lent night, ho - ly night,

All is calm, all is bright

Round yon vir - gin moth - er and child.

Ho - ly in - fant so ten - der and mild,

Sleep in heav - en - ly peace,___

Sleep___ in heav - en - ly peace. ___

The Friendly Beasts

Traditional English Carol

1. Je - sus, our broth - er, kind and good,
Was hum - bly born in a sta - ble rude,
And the friend - ly beasts a - round him stood;
Je - sus, our broth - er, kind and good.

2. "I," said the donkey, shaggy and brown,
"I carried his mother up hill and down;
I carried her safely to Bethlehem town.
I," said the donkey, shaggy and brown.

3. "I," said the cow, all white and red,
"I gave him my manger for a bed;
I gave him my hay to pillow his head.
I," said the cow, all white and red.

4. "I," said the sheep with curly horn,
   "I gave him my wool for his blanket warm;
   He wore my coat on Christmas morn.
   I," said the sheep with curly horn.

5. "I," said the dove from the rafters high,
   "I cooed him to sleep, that he should not cry;
   We cooed him to sleep, my mate and I.
   I," said the dove from the rafters high.

6. And every beast by some good spell,
   In the stable dark was glad to tell
   Of the gift he gave Emmanuel,
   The gift he gave Emmanuel.

Mary Had a Baby

Spiritual

Tenderly

1. Mar - y had a ba - by, Yes, Lord,

Mar - y had a ba - by, Yes, my Lord,

Mar - y had a ba - by, Yes, Lord,

The peo - ple keep a - com - ing and the train has gone.

2. What did Mary name him . . .
3. Mary named him Jesus . . .
4. Where was Jesus born . . .

5. Born in lowly stable . . .
6. Where did Mary lay him . . .
7. Laid him in a manger . . .

You can play an accompaniment for this song with just two tones.
Play this pattern three times,   then play this pattern once.

F   E   F

F   F   E   F

88

The Tiny Child

Colombian Carol
Words translated

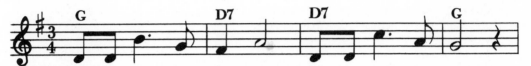

1. Come now lit - tle shep - herds, Come to Beth - le - hem.
   ¡Va - mos pas - tor - ci - tos! ¡Va - mos a Be - lén!
2. Now with hap - py sing - ing, Greet this bless - ed morn,

Come to see the Vir - gin and the ti - ny child.
A ver a la Vir - gen y al Ni - ño tam - bién.
And the ti - ny child __ who has just been born.

Gifts

by B.A.

Rubies, diamonds, emeralds, gold!
Satins, silk, shimmering bold,
Laid by His crib in a manger low!

Choose instruments to help express this poem.
Speak the poem with high, low, and solo voices.
Make up an accompaniment using the instruments you have chosen.

89

The Nutcracker Suite

by Peter Ilyich Tchaikovsky

This music helps dancers tell a story about a girl
who had a dream on Christmas Eve.

The orchestra plays an "Overture."

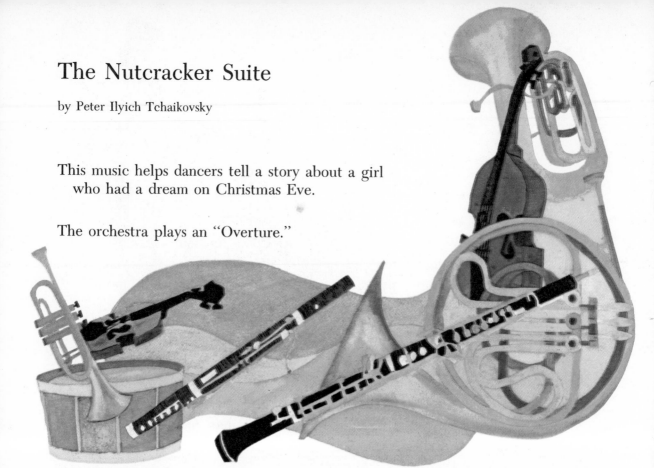

The guests enter to a "March."

The toys entertain.

The flowers dance.

Sounds of Harmony

HIGH Low tones played together make harmony

Can you hear harmony
  played by an orchestra?
  sung by a choir?

Can you make harmony
  when you play on the autoharp?
  when you play the bells?
  when you sing with friends?

The Little Green Fly and
The Little Black Bug

by Margaret Wise Brown

Little green fly, little green fly,
Where have you been?
I've been way up high,
Said the little green fly,
Bzzzzzzzzzz Bzzzzzzzzzz

Make up a melody that sounds like a fly "way up high."
Choose from these bells to make your melody.

Will you choose low bells or high bells?

Little black bug, little black bug,
Where have you been?
I've been under the rug,
Said the little black bug.
Bug-ug-ug-ug, Bug-ug-ug-ug

Ask someone else to make a melody that sounds like the
    black bug crawling under the rug.
Should he choose low bells or high bells?
Can the fly and the bug move at the same time?
Can you play your melodies at the same time?

93

Ingonyama

Zulu Folk Song

Which of these animals do you think is the best?
    Some say, "The lion is the bravest!"
    Others say, "But the hippo is the strongest!"
Begin the argument.
Chant the name of the animal you've chosen in this rhythm.

Some: The li - on,   The li - on,
Others: hip - po!   hip - po!

Two people may play the argument on the drum and wood block.
Others may join in the argument by singing this song.

Some: In - gon - ya - ma, gon - ya - ma, gon - ya - ma!

In - gon - ya - ma, gon - ya - ma, gon - ya - ma!

Others: In - voo - boo, voo - boo, voo - boo, in - voo - boo!

94

After School

Chinese Folk Tune
Translated by Grace Boynton

Listen to the recording of this song.
Listen for a pattern played on two bells.
Play the pattern and accompany the class.
Use these bells.

School is ___ out as the sun goes down;

Books in my bag I go through the town.

Here are my par - ents who smile at me;

I make a nice low bow like this: you see!

YOU CAN HEAR HARMONY

Listen to the recording of "The Angel Band."
Which of these instruments do you hear?

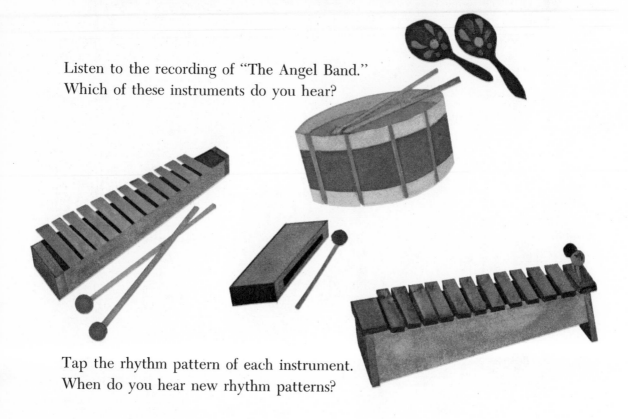

Tap the rhythm pattern of each instrument.
When do you hear new rhythm patterns?

The Angel Band

South Carolina Folk Song

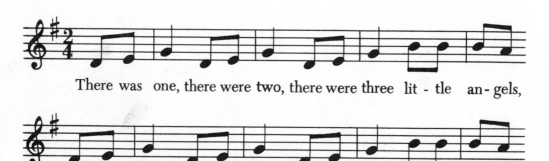

There was one, there were two, there were three lit - tle an - gels,

There were four, there were five, there were six lit - tle an - gels,

There were sev'n, there were eight, there were nine lit-tle an-gels,

Ten lit-tle __ an-gels in the band. _____

Refrain

Was-n't that a band, Sun - day morn - ing,

Sun - day morn - ing, Sun - day morn - ing?

Was-n't that a band, Sun - day morn - ing,

Sun - day morn - ing soon? _____

Mary Contrary

Words from Mother Goose
Music by B.A.

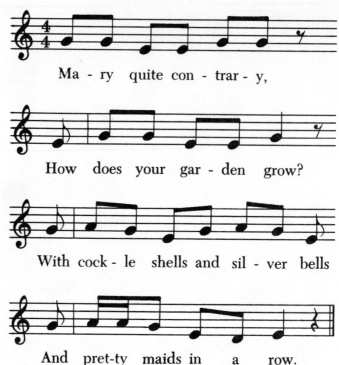

Ma - ry quite con - trar - y,

How does your gar - den grow?

With cock - le shells and sil - ver bells

And pret - ty maids in a row.

Add this special part to the song.

One pret-ty maid danced in the shade,

Two pret-ty maids with bells they played,

Three pret-ty maids with dreams to trade,

Four pret-ty maids with sticks they made.

Perform the song like this:

SONG   SPECIAL PART   SONG

Can someone add harmony? Play this piano accompaniment while the
class sings the song and special part.

Twelve Cypresses, B. 152

Cypress No. 11
by Antonin Dvořák

Listen to a string quartet.
Each intrument plays a special part.
Together they make harmony.

One violin plays a high melody.
The other violin, the viola, and the cello play patterns
   to accompany the melody.

Here is a picture of the first part of the music.
Can you follow the picture with your finger as you listen?
When do you hear the high melody begin?

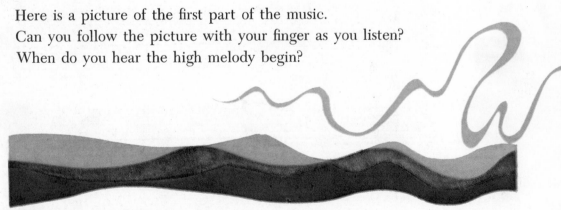

Listen to the whole composition.
Does the same instrument always play the melody?

John the Rabbit

American Folk Song

Oh John the Rab - bit oh yes,

Got a bad hab - it oh yes,

He's nib - bling in my gar - den oh yes,

Eat - ing up my tur - nips oh yes,

And my sweet po - ta - toes oh yes,

And my ripe to - ma - toes oh yes.

Well if I live ___ to see next fall,

My gar - den won't have ___ an - y vege - ta - bles at all.

Two people can play an accompaniment on the
   autoharp while the class sings.
One person may press down this chord button:
Press it down firmly.

The other person may strum the strings from low to high.
Strum with a steady beat.

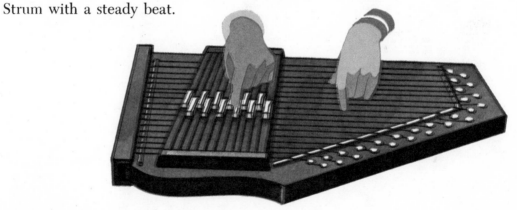

Here is a picture of the way your voices and the autoharp
   will sound in harmony.

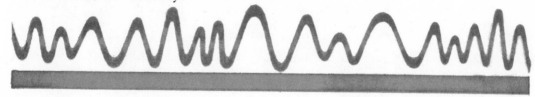

Goodbye Old Paint

American Folk Song

Swaying

Refrain   *Fine*

Good - bye, old Paint, I'm a - leav - in' Chey - enne.

Verse

1. My foot in the stir - rup, my po - ny won't stand. __
2. Old Paint's a good po - ny, he pa - ces when he can. __

D.C. al Fine

I'm a - leav - in' Chey - enne, I'm off for Mon - tan'. __
Good __ morn - ing, young lady, my hors - es won't stand. __

3. Oh, hitch up your hosses and feed 'em some hay,
   And seat yourself by me, as long as you stay.

4. I am a-riding old Paint, I am a-leading old Dan,
   I'm goin' to Montan' for to throw the hoolihan.

Repeat these parts many times as you sing the song.

Part 1 - Tone Blocks

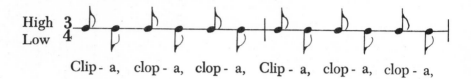

Clip - a,   clop - a,   clop - a,   Clip - a,   clop - a,   clop - a,

Part 2 - Piano or Xylophone

Part 3 - Bells

Part 4 - Bells

Part 5
Find a place to add jingle clogs for the sound of spurs.

Balancing Act

Sculpture by Earl Krentzin

Look at this sculpture.
What do you see first?
What else do you see?

When you look at sculpture, you can see several things at once.
When you listen to music, you can hear several things at once.

Compose music that suggests the things you see in the sculpture.
Two people may work together.

Use these bells for the acrobats.

Use these autoharp chords
   for the man on horseback.

What other instruments might you use?

104

Train Is A-Coming

Spiritual

1. Train is a - com - ing, Oh, yes,

Train is a - com - ing, ___ Oh, yes,

Train is a - com - ing, Train is a com - ing,

Train is a com - ing, Oh, yes.

2. Better get your ticket, Oh, yes, *(2 times)*
   Better get your ticket, *(2 times)*
   Better get your ticket, Oh, yes.

3. Train is a-leaving, Oh, yes *(2 times)*
   Train is a-leaving, *(2 times)*
   Train is a-leaving, Oh, yes.

Music Has Design

Can you **see** design?

    Can you find the little parts that make up a big picture?

    Are some parts more important than others?

    Are some parts repeated? Are others different?

Can you **hear** design?

    Can you hear the parts that make up a composition?

    Are some parts more important than others?

    Are some parts repeated? Are others different?

Be a Copycat

Here is a rhythm round.
    Linda Lee, can you be
    A copycat and follow me?

You have performed a rhythm round. Now listen to a
    melodic round on your recording.

Can you hear when each new instrument begins to play
    the same melody?

Do you recognize the melody?

The Cowboy

Old Texas Melody
Words by Mayme Christenson

Can you find the parts in this music?

Slide your finger along the cowboy's rope as you listen.

You should reach the cow at the end of each part of the music.

What helps you know when one part is ended?

Each part is called a **phrase.**

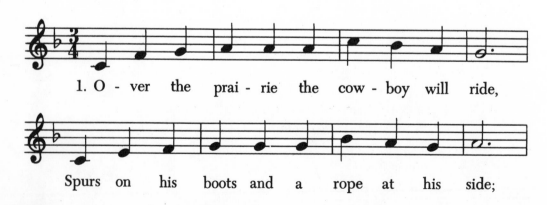

1. O - ver the prai - rie the cow - boy will ride,

Spurs on his boots and a rope at his side;

Far from the ranch house he trav - els each day,

Yip - pee - ki! Yip - pee - ki! Yip - pee - ki - yay!

2. Here he comes whirling the rope in his hand;
   Soon he will lasso the cattle to brand.
   Work now is over, he gallops away,
   Yip-pee-ki! Yip-pee-ki! Yip-pee-ki-yay!

3. Nighttime is falling, he opens his pack,
   Lays out his blanket and sleeps on his back,
   Saddle for pillow, no roof but the sky,
   Yip-pee-ki! Yip-pee-ki! Yip-pee-ki-yi!

Contradance

from *Divertimento No. 8 in F Major*

by Wolfgang Amadeus Mozart

Listen to this musical conversation.
Find a partner and dance a musical conversation.
One person begins with a short question, the other answers.

Sleigh Ride

Russian Folk Melody
Words by William S. Haynie

Choose a different instrument to accompany each phrase
  of this song.
How many instruments will you choose?

1. Come with me in win- try weath- er,
2. We will see the trot- ting hors- es

In our sleigh we'll ride. Oh!
As they pull the sleigh. Oh!

Wrap us tight so the wind won't bite;
Sing a song as we ride a - long;

Then o'er the snow we'll glide. Oh!
Come let's be on our way. Oh!

110

Honey, You Can't Love One

Traditional American Song

1. Hon - ey, you can't love one, _____

Hon - ey, you can't love one, _____

You can't love one and still have your fun,

Oh, Hon - ey, you can't love one. _____

2. Honey, you can't love two, *(2 times)*
   You can't love two and always be true,
   Oh, Honey, you can't love two.

3. Honey, you can't love three, *(2 times)*
   You can't love three and still go with me,
   Oh, Honey, you can't love three.

Can you add some new verses to this song?

4. Honey, you can't love four, *(2 times)*
   You can't love four and . . . . .
   Oh, Honey, you can't love four.

Shoemaker's Song

Danish Singing Game

Wind, wind, wind the bob-bin,
Roll, roll. roll the thread and

Wind, wind, wind the bob-bin,
Roll, roll, roll the thread and

Fine

Pull, pull, and tap, tap, tap.

Now we'll sew the right shoe O!

D.C. al Fine

Then we'll stitch the left just so.

Plan movements for each phrase of this dance.
Will you repeat any of your movements?

112

An Event for a Composer and a Performer

Choose a high and low bell with the same letter name.

Which letter did you choose?
Take the two bells out of the box.
How many different ways can you play them?

Can you play:

a high sound

a low sound

a soft sound

a loud sound

a silly sound

a long sound

a short sound

Plan a composition.
Draw the pictures to remind you when to play
  the different sounds.
Ask a friend to play your composition.

The Lotus

Japanese Folk Song

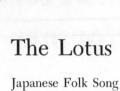

Four of you may be the lotus blossom.
Open one petal at a time.
A new petal opens as each new phrase begins.
When will all the petals close?

Let's o - pen, o - pen now.

Which flower shall we o - pen__ now?

Let us o - pen lo - tus__ flower,

But as soon as it is o - pen,

Quick- ly a - gain it clo - - - ses.

114

The Flag Goes By

Music by William S. Haynie
Words by Henry Holcomb Bennett

1. Hats off! Hats off! A - long the street there comes
2. Hats off! Hats off! A - long the street there comes

A blare of bu - gles, a ruf - fle of drums,
A blare of bu - gles, a ruf - fle of drums,

A flash of col - or be - neath the sky:
And loy - al hearts are ___ beat - ing high:

Hats off! Hats off! The flag is pass - ing by.
Hats off! Hats off! The flag is pass - ing by.

March around the room as you sing the song.
Listen for the phrases.
Turn around each time a phrase ends.

Some people may play an accompaniment.
What instruments would be good to use?
Each person should play a different rhythm pattern.

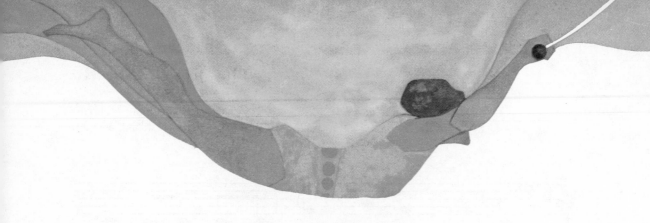

Man on the Flying Trapeze

Traditional American Song

Draw a curved line on the chalkboard as you hear each phrase.
Will you use the same color to draw every phrase?

He'd fly through the air with the great - est of ease,

This dar - ing young man on the fly - ing tra - peze,

His ac - tions are grace - ful, all girls he does please,

And my love he has sto - len a - way. _____

Haul Away, Joe

Sea Chantey

1. A - way, haul a - way, __ Come haul a - way to - geth - er;
2. A - way, haul a - way, __ I'll sing to you of Nan - cy;

A - way, haul a - way, __ Haul a - way, Joe.
A - way, haul a - way, __ Haul a - way, Joe.

A - way, haul a - way, __ We'll haul for bet - ter weath - er;
A - way, haul a - way, __ She's just my style and fan - cy;

A - way, haul a - way, __ We'll haul a - way Joe.
A - way, haul a - way, __ We'll haul a - way Joe.

Can you find any phrases that are **repeated?**

Dipidu

African Folk Song

This song has a puzzle.
The notes are missing from the second staff.
Listen to the recording.
Can you decide what note patterns should be there?

Slowly

Gui - dee,   a zi - ka - ku, Gui - dee,   a   dip - i - du.

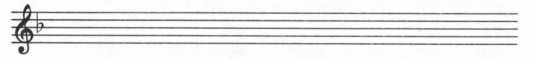

Gui - dee,   a zi - ka - ku, Gui - dee,   a   dip - i - du.

Dip, dip,   dip - i - du,   dip - i - du, a - dip - i - du.

Dip dip dip dip dip - i - du, dip - i - du, a - dip - i - du.

118

Boysie

Folk Song from Trinidad

Here is another puzzle.

Listen to the music. How many sections do you hear?

Look at the music. How many sections do you see?

Can you find the other section that you heard?

All I rock-a rock Boy-sie, Boy-sie wouldn't sleep.

Fine

All I rock-a rock Boy-sie, Boy-sie wouldn't sleep.

Go up-town, go down-town, meet Boy-sie there.

D.C. al Fine

Go up-town, go down-town, meet Boy-sie there.

The Choo Choo

Hungarian Children's Song

What color should be used to show the design of phrase 2?
Look at the music to help you decide.
Listen! Were you right?

There's the choo choo, there's the choo choo, Ka - ni - zsa line.

Ka - ni - zsa, oh, Ka - ni - zsa, oh, run - ning so fine.

En - gi - neer sits in the cab high,

Makes the choo choo, makes the choo choo rat - tle on by.

Used by permission of the Cooperative Recreation Service, Inc., Delaware, Ohio.

Prince of Denmark March

by Jeremiah Clarke

Look at this design of music shown with lines and colors.
Do you think you will hear parts in the music that sound
the same?
Will some parts sound almost the same?
Will some parts sound different?

Follow the design with your finger as you listen.
Be careful not to reach the end of each line too soon!

Donkey Small

Music by Norman Luboff
Words by Marilyn Keith
and Alan Bergman

This song has three big sections.
Can you decide when the second section begins?
What do you notice about the third section?

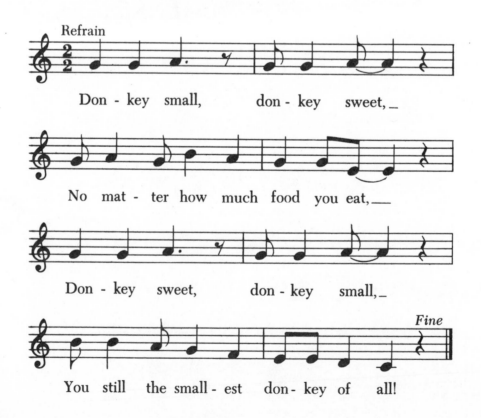

Refrain

Don - key small,   don - key   sweet, _

No mat - ter how much food you eat, __

Don - key sweet,   don - key   small, _

You still   the small - est don - key of   all!

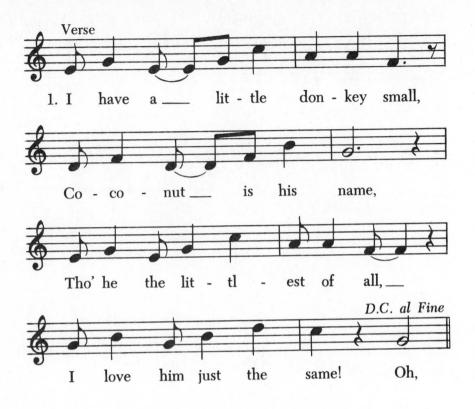

Verse

1. I have a ___ lit - tle don - key small,

Co - co - nut ___ is his name,

Tho' he the lit - tl - est of all, ___

D.C. al Fine

I love him just the same! Oh,

2. I have a little donkey small,
   He makes me laugh all day!
   His ears go up when him I call,
   Coconut love to play!
   Refrain

3. Up on his back I ride to town,
   Sometime he make me late,
   All of a sudden he sit down,
   I have to stand and wait!
   Refrain

Expression in Music

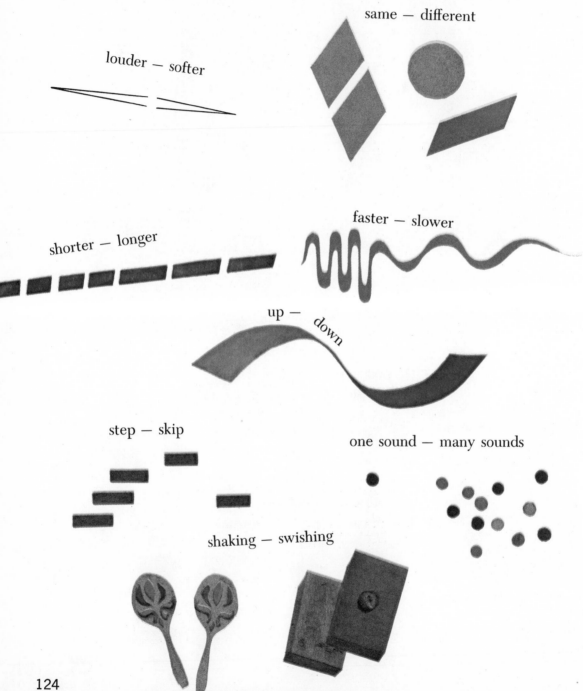

louder — softer

same — different

shorter — longer

faster — slower

up — down

step — skip

one sound — many sounds

shaking — swishing

Sounds Express Feelings

Can you tell how a person feels by looking at him?

Can you tell how a person feels by hearing him talk?

Can you tell someone how you feel by using musical sounds?

Choose a word that describes a feeling.

Make up music to describe that feeling.

Ask your friends to listen. Can they guess the word you chose?

Rainy Day

Words and Music
by Virginia Stroh Red

Have you ever sat inside on a rainy day and watched the rain?
How did you feel?
Listen to the music on the recording.
Does it help express the feelings you had?
What did the composer do to help express these feelings?

Lightly and steadily

Watch the rain - drops fall,

It seems they want to play.

They chase each oth - er down the pane,

Slip - slid - ing all the way.

SOUNDS TELL STORIES

Make up sounds to describe a rain shower.

Tell this story with your sounds.

You may want to use some of your sounds as an introduction at the
beginning of "Rainy Day" or as a coda at the end of the song.

Posheen, Posheen, Posho

Words and Music by John Jacob Niles

Listen to the recordings of "Posheen, Posheen, Posho" and "Firefly."
How do the performers help tell the story?

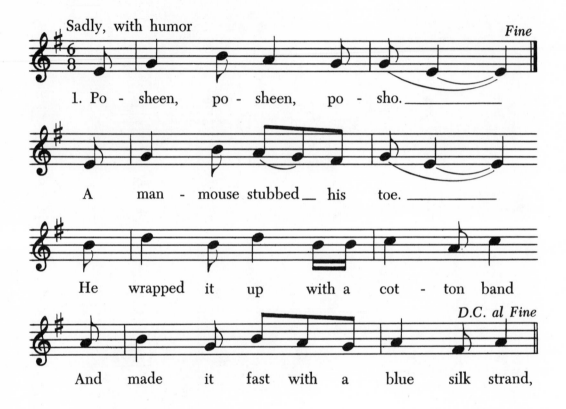

Sadly, with humor

1. Po - sheen, po - sheen, po - sho.

A man - mouse stubbed his toe.

He wrapped it up with a cot - ton band

And made it fast with a blue silk strand,

2. Posheen, posheen, posho,
   A girl-mouse laughèd so
   To see a man-mouse with a wrappèd up toe.
   She laughed ho, ho, ho, ho, ho, ho, ho. . . . .

3. Posheen, posheen, posho,
   Her granny was angered so.
   She plucked a stem of yellow broom corn
   And with a will she laid it on. . . . .

Firefly

Croatian Air
Words by
Elizabeth Madox Roberts

1. A lit - tle light is go - ing by,
2. I nev - er could have thought of it,

A lit - tle light is go - ing __ by,
I nev - er could have thought __ of __ it,

Is go - ing up to see the sky,
To have a lit - tle bug all lit,

1.
A lit - tle light __ with __ wings.

2.
And made to go __ on __ wings,

on wings.

Sound Is a Moving Thing

When air moves through a pipe,
it makes a *whirring* sound.

When air moves in the tail of a jet plane,
it makes a ROARING sound.

When air moves through your lips,
it can make a *whistling* sound.

When air moves through lips into a brass instrument,
it makes a *musical* sound.

Listen to brass instruments on your recording of "The Flag Goes By."
How many different brass instruments do you hear?

Sound Is a Moving Thing

When air moves through a   there is the sound of rustling leaves.

When air moves through a

there is the sound of rattling shutters.

When air moves through

there is the sound of crackling reeds.

When you blow air through a woodwind instrument,

there is a musical sound.

Listen to woodwind instruments on your recording of "Carrousel."
Do all these instruments sound the same?

Sound Is a Moving Thing

What moves to make sound when you hear:

a bat hit a ball?

a spoon hit a pan?

sticks hit a drum?

a beater hit a gong?

mallets hit a xylophone?

Which of these sounds are made on percussion instruments?
Which percussion instruments can you hear on your recording of
"Percussion Melee" by Rudolph Ganz?

Sound Is a Moving Thing

What moves to make sound . . . .

when you thump a stretched rubber band?

when you shoot an arrow?

when you spin a yoyo?

when you bow a string instrument?

Listen to "Circle Around."
In which part of the music do you hear only string instruments?

Mala Suite

by Witold Lutoslawski

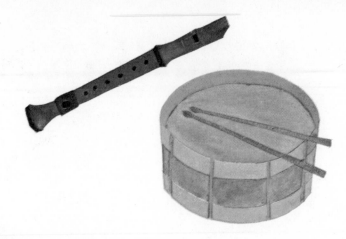

Wooden Flute

Can you whistle?
Can you echo my whistle?

Listen as the "Wooden Flute" seems to whistle too. It plays a
   high piping melody.

Drums, strings, and brass instruments often interrupt by playing
   short, loud sounds.

Can you hear the flute echo the sounds of the louder instruments?

Can you whistle the last three tones of this piece? The first
   three tones?

Jolly Polka

"Hurray! Hurray! Fun and dancing have begun!"
Dance to this music!
Will you dance fast or slow?

Dance with the different instruments as they play the tune.

Very Small Song

Listen to this very small song.
Can you hear one instrument play?
    Two instruments play?
        More instruments play?

Does this piece end loudly or softly?
What words can you use to describe this composition?

Dance

Can you use movement to express the changes in this dance?
When will your movements be short and quick?
When will they be smooth and flowing?

What Do I Hear?

Stop! Listen!
What do I hear?
Away at a distance
Now it comes near.

Away at a distance < **Now it comes near.**

What will come near?

Right on our sidewalk
Just hear him play
Here comes a drummer
Parading today.

Right through my window
Just hear it moan.
Here comes the wind,
A mournful tone.

Choose sounds to help answer the question.
What would happen to the story if the sound looked like this?

I'm Gonna Sing

Spiritual

Sing the song softly.
Sing the song loudly.
Get softer as you sing some parts.
Get louder as you sing other parts.

Show the way you sang.
Use the signs you found on page 136.

1. I'm gon - na sing when the Spir - it says "Sing,"____
2. I'm gon - na shout when the Spir - it says "Shout," __

I'm gon - na sing when the Spir - it says "Sing," __
I'm gon - na shout when the Spir - it says "Shout," _

I'm gon - na sing when the Spir - it says "Sing," ____
I'm gon - na shout when the Spir - it says "Shout," ____

And o - bey the Spir - it of the Lord. ____
And o - bey the Spir - it of the Lord. ____

All the Pretty Little Horses

American Folk Song

What kind of song is "All the Pretty Little Horses"?
How can you express its **mood** as you sing? As you play
   an accompaniment?

Hush - a - by, don't you cry,

Go to sleep-y, lit - tle ba - by.

When you wake, you shall have

All the pret - ty lit - tle hors - es:

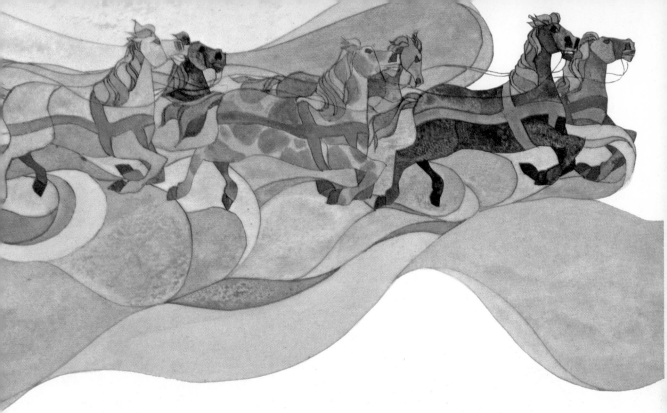

Blacks and bays, dap - ples and grays,

Coach and six - a lit - tle hors - es.

pp Hush - a - by, don't you cry,

Go to sleep - y, lit - tle ba - by.

Carnival of the Animals

by Camille Saint-Saens

If you were a composer, how would you describe these animals in music?

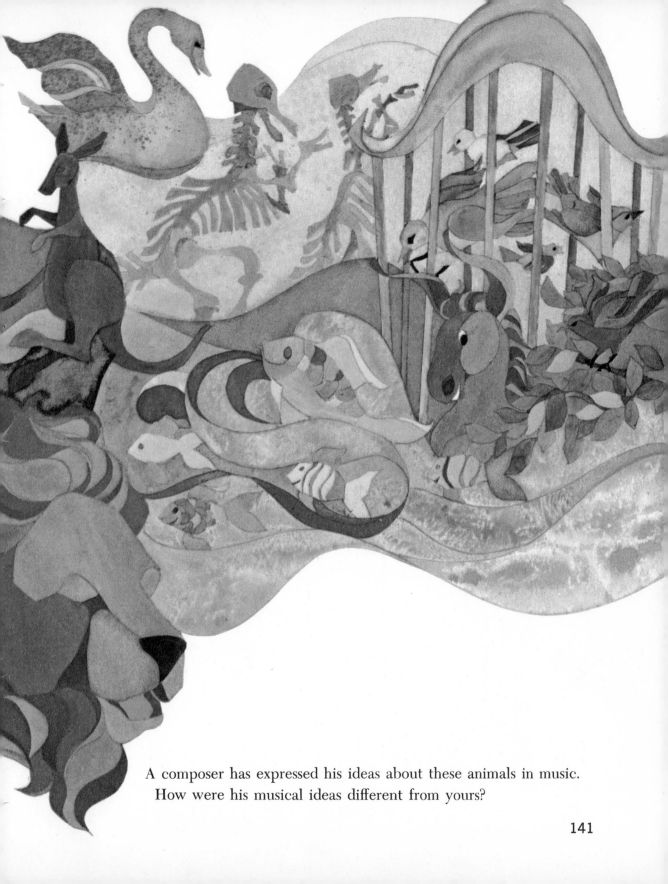

A composer has expressed his ideas about these animals in music.
How were his musical ideas different from yours?

141

Boom Dali Da

Israeli Folk Song

Listen to the recording. What helps make the music exciting?
Listen again. As the tempo gets faster or slower,
 point to the matching picture.

Slow   Fast   Getting Faster   Getting Slower

Slowly

Boom da-li da, Boom da-li da, Boom da-li, da-li,

very fast

Boom da-li, da-li, Boom da-li, da-li, Boom da-li, da-li,

Boom, ha! ha! Boom da-li, da-li, Boom da-li, da li, Boom!

Da - li, da - li, da, Boom!

Go Tell Aunt Rhodie

American Folk Song

Read the words of the song.

When you are singing, should the tempo be fast? Slow?
    Always the same?

1. Go tell Aunt Rho - die, Go tell Aunt Rho - die,

Go tell Aunt Rho - die, The old gray goose is dead.

2. The one she's been saving, The one she's been saving,
   The one she's been saving, To make a feather bed.

3. She died in the mill pond, She died in the mill pond,
   She died in the mill pond, Standing on her head.

4. The goslings are crying, The goslings are crying,
   The goslings are crying, The old gray goose is dead.

5. The gander is weeping, The gander is weeping,
   The gander is weeping, The old gray goose is dead.

143

Three Pirates

Old English Sea Chantey

1. Three pi - rates came to Lon - don Town,

Yo - ho! _____ Yo - ho! _____

Three pi - rates came to Lon - don Town,

Yo - ho! _____ Yo - ho! _____

Three pi - rates came to Lon - don Town,

To see the King put on his crown,

Yo - ho,   you lub - bers! Yo - ho,   you lub - bers!

Yo - ho!   Yo - ho!   Yo - ho!

2. They came upon a wayside inn, Yo-ho! Yo-ho! *(2 times)*
   They came upon a wayside inn,
   And said, "Good landlord let us in."
   Yo-ho, you lubbers! Yo-ho, you lubbers!
   Yo-ho! Yo-ho! Yo-ho!

3. "O landlord you have lots of gold," Yo-ho! Yo-ho! *(2 times)*
   "O landlord you have lots of gold,
   Enough to fill the after hold."
   Yo-ho, you lubbers! Yo-ho, you lubbers!
   Yo-ho! Yo-ho! Yo-ho!

Act out this story as you sing.
Add musical sounds to help express the ideas.

145

More Music to Explore

rhythm   melody patterns   voices   coda

phrase   section   instruments

accompaniment   introduction   tempo   sounds

scale

repeat   design   composition

silence

harmony

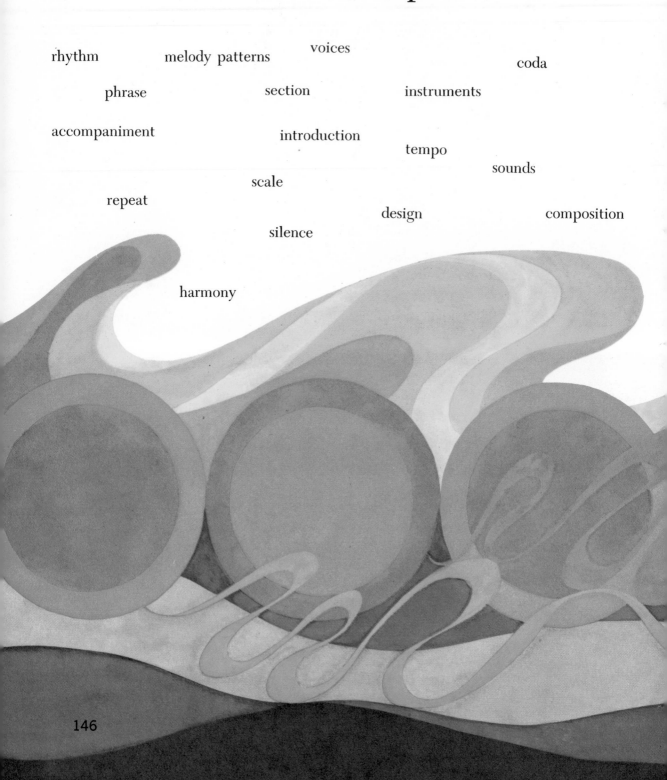

Describe
Find
Show
Make
Music

Read the words on page 146.
These are music words you have learned this year.
Can you **describe** what each means?
Can you **find** music that shows what each word means?

Can you **make** your own music to show what the words mean?

Spring Song

Chinese Folk Song
English Words Adapted

Spring brings the sun __ where the win - ter has lain,

Spring brings the com - fort of warm gen - tle rain,

Spring brings song - birds from far a - way,

"Win - ter's gone now," they seem to __ say,

Spring- time has brought us this bright new __ day.

Play this accompaniment on the finger cymbals.

Morning Song

American Folk Hymn
Words by Jane Rolfe Randolph

Expressively

1. Dawn is like a __ gate that o - pens

On a mead - ow __ wide and fair.

Through the o - pen gate I hur - ry;

Gold - en light __ is __ ev - ery - where.

2. Up and down that pleasant meadow
   There are other children too.
   Games we have and work and singing;
   In a day there's much to do.

3. Dawn is like a gate that opens
   On a meadow wide and bright.
   Through the gate I hurry singing,
   Out into the golden light.

Words by Jane Rolfe Randolph, from *New Music Horizons*, Fifth
Book, copyright 1946, 1953 by Silver Burdett Company. Used
by permission.

SUMMER IS A TIME FOR PLAYING

Some composers have written music about children at play.

Tag

from *Summer Day Suite*

by Serge Prokofieff

Do you think this music will be fast or slow?
Will the melodies have only a few tones, or will they have
   many tones?
Listen to the music. Did it move as you thought it would?
How did the instruments seem to play tag?

The Pines of Villa Borghese

from *The Pines of Rome*

by Ottorino Respighi

Have you ever teased a friend by chanting like this?

Ha! Ha! You can't catch me! Ha! Ha! You can't catch me!

Can you hear this chant in the music?

150

Praeludium

by Armas Jarnefelt

Listen to this merry melody. Could this be a happy walking tune?
Could it be a time to gather friends as you go?

Imagine that everyone is together arm in arm. Can you hear the
strings play the happy tune?

The first melody returns, and everyone is off to gather more friends.

Can you hear when everyone seems to stop and look at the quiet
beauty of the summer day?

The piece ends as all walk away . . . . . to find more friends, of course!

March

from *Summer Day Suite*

by Serge Prokofieff

Is this a stately march for kings and queens?
Is it a soldier's march?
Is it a playful march?
Can you follow this melody from the march?

I Hear the Mill-Wheel

French-Canadian Folk Song

I hear the mill - wheel, tick - a tick - a tack - a,

Fine

I hear the mill - wheel, tack - a.

My fa - ther's build - ing me a house,

I hear the mill - wheel, tack - a.

Car - pen - ters three work on my house,

D.C. al Fine

Tick - a tack - a, tick - a tack - a.

Rique Ran

Latin-American Folk Song

A - se - rrín,   a - se - rrán,

All   the   woods - men   of   San   Juan

Eat   their   cheese   and   eat   their   pan,

Those from Ri - que   al - fe - ñi - que;

Those from Ro - que   al - fon - do - que,

Ri - qui,   ri - que,   ri - qui   ran.

Point to the pictures of the instruments which play the **melody.**

Point to the pictures of the instruments which
play **rhythm patterns.**

153

The Lollipop Tree

Music by George Kleinsinger
Words by Joe Darion

Spirited

1. One fine day in ear - ly spring I played a fun - ny trick,
2. Then one day I woke to find a ver - y love - ly sight,
3. Win - ter came and days grew cold as win - ter days will do,

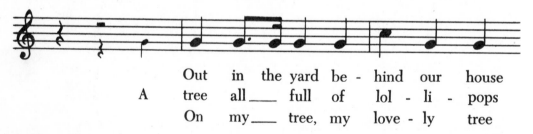

Out   in the yard be - hind our   house
A   tree   all___ full of   lol - li - pops
On   my___ tree, my   love - ly   tree

I   plant - ed   a   lol - li - pop   stick,
had   grown   in   the   dark___ of   night,
not   one   lit - tle   lol - li - pop   grew,

Then ev - ery day I wa - tered it well
I sat be - neath that won - der - ful tree
From ev - ery branch an i - ci - cle hung,

and watched it care - ful - ly,
and looked up with a grin,
the twigs were bare as bones,

I hoped one day that stick would grow
And when I o - pened up my mouth
But when I broke the i - ci - cles off

to   be   a   lol - li - pop   tree;
a   pop   would   drop ___ right   in;
they   turned   to   ice - cream   cones;

Ha, ha, ha,   Ho, ho, ho,   What   a   sight   to   see,
Ha, ha, ha,   Ho, ho, ho,   What   a   place   to   be,
Ha, ha, ha,   Ho, ho, ho,   How   I   danced with glee,

Me   and   my   lol - li - pop,   lol - li - pop,   lol - li - pop,
Un - der   a   lol - li - pop,   lol - li - pop,   lol - li - pop,
Un - der   the   lol - li - pop,   lol - li - pop,   lol - li - pop,

lol - li,   lol - li,   lol - li - pop   tree.
lol - li,   lol - li,   lol - li - pop   tree.
lol - li,   lol - li,   lol - li - pop   tree.

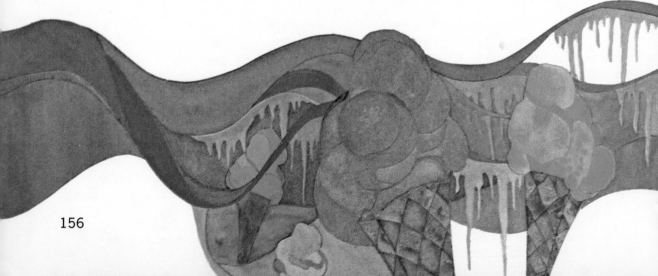

Winter Is Over

Italian-Swiss Folk Tune
English Words
by Katherine R. Rohrbough

1. The win-ter now is o - ver and A - pril rains are past;

I know I heard this morn-ing the cuck-oo's song at last.

Cuck-oo!   Cuck-oo!   Oh, can't you hear it too?

I know I heard this morn-ing the cuck-oo's song at last.

2. The sun on every mountain has melted winter's snow;
   The birds build in the tree tops, the cuckoo's call they know.

There Was Once a Princess

Spanish and Latin-American Folk Song

There was once a prin - cess beau - ti - ful,

There was once a prin - cess beau - ti - ful,

When so few of such were seen, _____

When so few of such were seen.

Someone may add a new section to this song.

The prin - cess was _____ ___ ___ ___ ___ ___

The prin - cess wore..

End the song by repeating the first section.

158

Calico Pie

Words and Music by Norman Cazden
Adapted from a poem by Edward Lear

1. Cal - i - co pie, the lit - tle birds fly
2. Cal - i - co jam, the lit - tle fish swam

Down to the cal - i - co tree; _____
O - ver the cal - i - co sea. _____

Their wings so blue that they sing, til - la - loo,
He doffed his hat to the sole and the sprat,

And they nev - er come back _____ to me, to me,
And he nev - er came back _____ to me, to me,

And they nev - er come back _____ to me. _____
And he nev - er came back _____ to me. _____

For the Beauty of the Earth

Music by Conrad Kocher
Words by Folliott S. Pierpont

1. For the beau - ty of the earth,
2. For the won - der of each hour

For the beau - ty of the skies,
Of the day and of the night,

For the love which from our birth
Hill and vale, and tree and flow'r,

O - ver and a - round us lies,
Sun and moon, and stars of light,

Lord of all, to thee we raise

This our hymn of grate - ful praise.

Let's Explore Art

Senecio, Paul Klee. Offentliche Kunstsammlung Basel, Switzerland.
Permission S.P.A.D.E.M. 1974 by French Reproduction Rights, Inc.

Let's Explore Art

In art you enjoy seeing familiar things.
Artists help you to see these things in new ways.

Look at the works of art in your book.
Can you see colors and lines?
Can you see rhythm and patterns and designs?

Discover different materials artists use.
Choose interesting materials and create art of your own.

Several Circles, No. 323, 1926, Vasily Kandinsky (1866-1944, Russia, Germany)
Oil on canvas. The Solomon R. Guggenheim Museum Collection, New York.

This painting is based on a pattern of repeated circles.
How does the artist give the painting variety?

The Merry Jesters, 1906, Henri Rousseau (1844-1910, France) Oil on
canvas. Philadelphia Museum of Art: The Louise and Walter Arensberg Collection.

What patterns do you see?
How did the artist form these patterns?
How does the painting help us imagine the deep, dark jungle?

Family Group, 1945-1949
(cast 1950),
Henry Moore (1898-
England) Bronze.
Collection: The Museum of
Modern Art, New York.
A. Conger Goodyear Fund.

Each artist creates in his own special way.
He chooses materials he likes.
He decides on a subject.
He uses imagination to create the work.

Man Pointing, 1947,
Alberto Giacometti (1901-1966,
Switzerland, France)
Bronze.
London: The Tate Gallery.

Figure, 1926-1930, Jacques Lipchitz
(1891-   , Lithuania) Bronze.
Collection: The Museum of Modern Art,
New York. Van Gogh Purchase Fund.

166

Vase of Flowers, Jan Davidsz. de Heem (1606-1683, Holland) Oil.
National Gallery of Art, Washington, D.C. Andrew Mellon Fund.

How many main colors do you see in the *Vase of Flowers?*
Why do you think the white flower is placed where it is?

Alexander and the Talking Tree, Leaf from a Persian manuscript, 1425. (MS. Ouseley Add. 176, fol. 311v).
Courtesy, The Curators of the Bodleian Library, Oxford.

Animals at Play (Choju Giga), Heian period (c. 800-1200) Sumi on paper.
Benrido Company, Ltd., Kyōto.

Leopard and Serpent, Antoine Louis Barye
(1796-1875, France). Watercolor.
The Metropolitan Museum of Art, New York.
Bequest of Mrs. H. O. Havemeyer,
1929. The H. O. Havemeyer Collection.

She-Goat, 1950, Pablo
Picasso (1881-1973, Spain,
France) Bronze (cast 1952).
Collection: The Museum of
Modern Art, New York.
Mrs. Simon Guggenheim Fund.

Tunk Mountains, Autumn, Maine, 1945, John Marin (1870-1953,
United States) Watercolor. The Phillips Collection, Washington, D.C.

In the paintings on these two pages, what lines and patterns do you see?
Look through your book at all the pictures of animals and birds.
Notice the different ways artists draw and paint to show their impressions.

The White Horse, 1898, Paul Gauguin (1848-1903, France, Peru, Tahiti)
Oil on canvas. The Louvre, Paris.

Carousel at Nahant, Detail, Maurice Prendergast (1859-1924, United States)
Watercolor. Courtesy, Museum of Fine Arts, Springfield, Massachusetts.

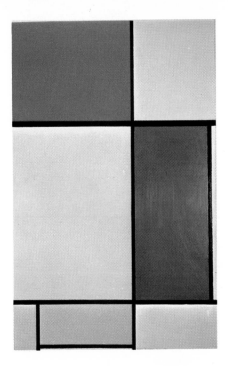

Large Composition in Red, Blue, and Yellow, 1928, Piet Mondrian (1872-1944, Holland, United States) Oil. Collection: Mr. and Mrs. Thomas Solley, Indiana. Courtesy, Sidney Janis Gallery, New York.

You know rhythm in music.
How do these artists create rhythm with lines?
How does the painting on page 172 suggest rhythm?
What designs do you see?

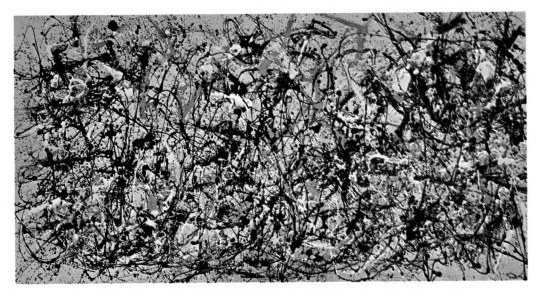

Autumn Rhythm, Jackson Pollock (1912-1956, United States) Oil on canvas. The Metropolitan Museum of Art, New York. George A. Hearn Fund, 1957.

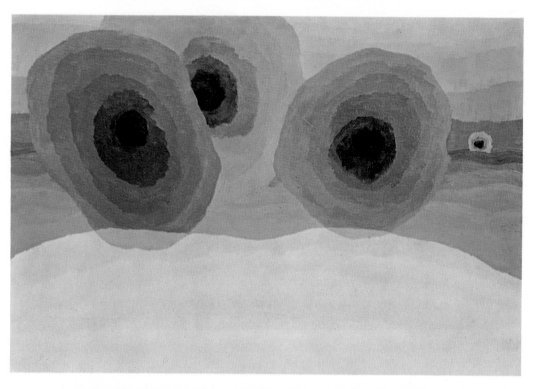

Fog Horns, Arthur Dove (1880-1946, United States) Oil.
Collection of the Colorado Springs Fine Arts Center, Colorado Springs.
Gift of Oliver B. James.

How did the artist use his imagination to create this painting?
Use your imagination. Think of other sounds you might paint in a picture.
Create a sound picture of your own.

Italian Comedians, Antoine Watteau (1684-1721, France) Oil on canvas. National Gallery of Art, Washington, D.C. Samuel H. Kress Collection.

People in many countries around the world like this painting. What do you think to be the reasons?

The Circus, 1891, Georges Seurat (1859-1891). Oil on canvas,
Louvre, Paris.

Classified Index

178

Alphabetical Index of Music and Poetry